MAINE OUTDOOR
ADVENTURE GUIDE

MAINE OUTDOOR ADVENTURE GUIDE

JOHN CHRISTIE AND JOSH CHRISTIE

Camden, Maine

Published by Down East Books
A wholly owned subsidiary of The Rowman & Littlefield Publishing Group, Inc.
4501 Forbes Boulevard, Suite 200, Lanham, Maryland 20706
www.rowman.com

Unit A, Whitacre Mews, 26–34 Stannary Street, London SE11 4AB

Distributed by NATIONAL BOOK NETWORK

British Library Cataloguing in Publication Information Available

Library of Congress Cataloging-in-Publication Data
Christie, John, 1937–
   Maine outdoor adventure guide / John Christie and Josh Christie.
      pages cm
   ISBN 978-1-60893-267-2 (pbk. : alk. paper)—ISBN 978-1-60893-268-9 (electronic)
1. Outdoor recreation—Maine. 2. Adventure and adventurers—Maine. 3. Wilderness
areas—Recreational use—Maine. 4. Maine—Guidebooks. I. Christie, Josh. II. Title.
   GV191.42.M2C47 2015
   796.509741—dc23

                                                                    2015016305

∞™ The paper used in this publication meets the minimum requirements of
American National Standard for Information Sciences—Permanence of Paper for
Printed Library Materials, ANSI/NISO Z39.48-1992.

Printed in the United States of America

CONTENTS

Part I: On Foot

Ease Into the Hiking Season   3

Bald Mountain   5

Exploring Great Wass Island   7

For a Hot Summer Hike, Hit the Ski Slopes   9

Beautiful Bigelow   13

Hidden in the Hundred Mile Wilderness   17

Hiking (and Fishing) Snow Mountain   21

The Borestone Mountain Audubon Sanctuary: The Perfect Fall Hike   23

Ladder Hikes Are a Step Up in Acadia   25

Gilsland Farm: A Gem Hidden in Plain Sight   27

Hiking on Campobello   29

Jewell Falls: A Special Place in the Fore River Sanctuary   33

Plenty to Please Near Damariscotta River   35

Rangeley's Range of Outdoor Activities   37

Something for Everyone on Tumbledown   39

Get a Look at Fall's Finery   41

Part II: On the Water

Back on the Bay   47

Androscoggin Adventure   49

Paddling Merchant's Row   51

Paddling the Chain of Ponds   55

Delightful Donnell Pond   57

Paddling the Magalloway and Androscoggin Rivers   59

Fun in Friendship   63

On the Harraseeket River   65

Paddling the Pemaquid River   67

Kayaking Cape Rosier   69

Muscongus Sound   73

Penobscot Bay Pearls   75

Prime Time for Rollin' on the River   77

Rediscovering Deboullie   79

Sandy River Ponds   81

Part III: On Wheels, Combination Trips, and Alternatives

A Day on Dyer Neck   85

One Day, Two Mountains, and Two Lakes   87

Petit Manan Wildlife Refuge   89

Kayaking (and Biking and Hiking) Cape Jellison   93

A Day on the Quiet Side   95

Beautiful Bike Rides for Every Ability   97

Down East Getaway   99

Wondrous Waterfalls   103

Biking the Casco Bay Islands   107

Portland Beaches—by Bicycle   109

Rock Climbing: Up, Up, and Away   113

Tunk Mountain   115

Spectacular Schoodic Peninsula   117

The Wonderful Abundance of Port Clyde   119

St. Andrews By-the-Sea   121

So Many Adventures Await   123

ON FOOT

I

Ease Into the Hiking Season

IDON'T KNOW ABOUT YOU, but I need to ease my way into summer hiking season here in Maine. Despite a winter spent in Maine's outdoors, my legs don't hit the month of June ready for miles and miles of through hikes. Before I get to the business of serious hiking, I like to spend my mornings and weekends on some shorter trails.

In southern Maine, there are plenty of local hikes that provide impressive views without much effort. Trips up Ossipee Hill, Sabattus Mountain, and Blueberry Mountain all top out at five miles or less, making them short, family-friendly day hikes. All three are also a relatively quick trip from Portland, which means you can summit and be back with plenty of time to catch the Sea Dogs.

Ossipee Hill (sometimes charitably called Ossipee Mountain) is in Waterboro, just beyond Gorham if you're headed west from Portland. The 1,058-foot summit is home to a Maine Forest Service fire tower, and on a clear day offers spectacular views of the Atlantic to the east and Mount Washington to the west.

To reach the trail up Ossipee Hill, hikers can follow McLucas Road in Waterboro. The road changes from pavement to dirt after only about 0.4 miles. The rocky road continues for 1.7 miles before hitting a rusted yellow gate, beyond which is the summit of Ossipee. Folks with good high-clearance, four-wheel-drive vehicles can actually drive up McLucas all the way to the gate, but the road is in pretty rough shape.

I'd recommend hiking from the bottom of McLucas Road. From there the hike to the summit is 2.3 miles each way. (From the yellow gate, it's a steep half-mile trip to the summit.) The peak is mostly bare rock, and houses radio towers, a few buildings, and the 35-foot wooden fire tower.

The 1,253-foot Sabattus Mountain is just off Route 5 in Lovell. It's the shortest hike of this trio—less than a mile each way—but offers plenty of oomph thanks to a near-vertical cliff at the summit. There are also attractions geological and biological for families, among them an impressive white quartz deposit and loads of local wildlife.

From Route 5 in Lovell, hikers need only follow the (sensibly named) Sabattus Mountain Road and Sabattus Trail Road to reach the trailhead. The loop trail, maintained by the Maine Bureau of Parks and Greater Lovell Land Trust, is both well-marked and well-traveled. Yellow blazes mark the entire loop trail. I suggest taking the left-hand trail going up, and descending via the right-hand side.

With a total elevation gain of only 500 feet, the summit of Sabattus can be reached without breaking a sweat. From the top, there are spectacular views to the south and west, showcasing the mountains of neighboring New Hampshire. A much-appreciated bench also happens to sit on the summit. One word of warning—the view is thanks to a sheer cliff that forms Sabattus's southwestern face, so families should take caution.

While the best-known peaks of the Bethel region are the eight that make up Sunday River, there are other notable mountains. There are many trails in the 12,000-acre Caribou-Speckled Mountain Wilderness; one of my favorites is a quick jaunt up Blueberry Mountain. The hike packs loads of attractions into a short distance, including waterfalls, rock slides, and a swimming hole.

To hike Blueberry Mountain, hikers can begin at the Bickford Brook Trail. The trail starts at the Brickett Place, a nineteenth-century brick farmhouse on Route 113 in Stow. Just shy of a mile up Bickford Brook, a sign directs hikers to the right to follow the Blueberry Ridge Trail. The next mile treats hikers to flumes, huge boulders, waterfalls, and views of rock slides. The trail continues its brief, steep ascent to the summit. From here a return down the trail provides for an easy three-mile round-trip.

For those looking for a longer journey, the Ridge Trail climbs north along a ridgeline. The up-and-down trail flits from wooded surroundings to wide-open overlooks, with peaks marked by cairns. After two miles, the Blueberry Ridge Trail rejoins the Bickford Brook Trail just below the peak of Ames Mountain. From here a left turn will take hikers to their vehicle via the Bickford Brook Trail, making for a seven-mile loop.

Have the energy for another summit? A spur at the junction spans the half-mile to the peak of 2,906-foot Speckled Mountain.

Short as these hikes are, they pack some serious scenic punch. They're a perfect way to get geared up for a fantastic hiking season in Maine.

Bald Mountain

BALD MOUNTAIN IN OQUOSSOC should be at the top of every hiker's summer must-do list. There's more than one Bald Mountain in Maine; this one sits in a prime location on a relatively narrow piece of land between Rangeley Lake to the east and Mooselookmeguntic Lake to the west.

Lost to history is a short-lived ski area on its north side that was a precursor to the halcyon days of winter recreation development in the 1960s in Maine and beyond. Competition from Saddleback and Sugarloaf, combined with its remote location caused the Bald Mountain Skiway to close within ten years. But the bad news for skiers turned out to be good news for hikers, as the ski trails are no longer evident, yet the classic north woods experience is there to be enjoyed by all.

Bald Mountain has earned its rightful place on every list of Maine's best and most popular hikes for a variety of reasons. First, the exertion to reward ratio equals such delightful climbs as Borestone, the Camden Hills, and many of the trails in Acadia. On a hike of less than an hour, over moderately difficult terrain at worst, you're rewarded with one of Maine's great scenic vistas.

To the west, Mooselookmeguntic, Richardson, Cupsuptic, and Umbagog Lakes shimmer in the summer sun, and mountains loom along the western horizon, stretching from Mt. Washington to Old Speck and Sunday River, up to Elephant, Bemis, Aziscoos, and West Kennebago Mountains. Looking north and east from the sturdy fire tower platform on the summit, your eye takes in East Kennebago, Bigelow, Sugarloaf, Crocker, Spaulding, Abraham, and Saddleback Mountains, as well as dozens of lesser peaks. And every vista is framed with blue water in the foreground provided by the legendary Rangeley Lakes.

That's the reward. As far as the exertion goes, the trail, which originates at a well-marked parking lot about a mile to the left from Haines Landing at the northern terminus of Route 4, can also be accessed from a parking lot just before you reach the Landing—but that route results in a slightly longer hike. The trail is about 1.3 miles long, and is divided into three distinct sections. The first third is a stroll through mixed hardwood with only a slight elevation gain, followed by a section of moderate pitch, but an easy climb. The final third is more of a scramble over rocks and boulders (keep your eye out for blue blazes so you can be sure to stay on the trail), ending at the fire tower on the exposed summit.

Combining a Bald Mountain hike with any of the dozens of other reasons to visit the Rangeley region makes for the perfect summer getaway—for example, you might want to pop your canoe or kayak into the nearby Cupsuptic River at a public boat launch just a few miles west of Oquossoc on Route 16 for a soothing paddle.

Exploring Great Wass Island

G REAT WASS ISLAND PROJECTS farther out to sea than any other landmass in eastern Maine, which is the principal reason it's a nature lover's dream. Combine that with 1,540 acres of land preserved by the Nature Conservancy, the remote location that's well off the traditional beaten path, and the prototypical working harbors of Jonesport and Beals, and a visit to the Great Wass Island Preserve should certainly be on your summer to-do list.

Great Wass is the home of legendary generations of boatbuilders, including one Vinal Beal, the craftsman who built cedar on oak Jonesport lobster boats, distinguished by their high prow and a narrow beam that turn the boat into the wind when the engine idles, making trap hauling that much easier. The 1949 vintage boat that we owned for years provoked us to head east a few decades ago for the lobster boat races down Moosabec Reach and under the bridge connecting Jonesport and Beals. We drank in the local color and discovered Great Wass Island.

A right turn onto Route 187 just past Columbia Falls on Route 1 will take you to Jonesport. Then you cross the bridge to Beals Island, followed by a causeway to Great Wass. The parking lot for the preserve is well-marked on the Great Wass Island Road, and from there you can explore on foot the spectacular property that comprises almost all of the southern part of the town of Beals.

Acquired by the Maine Chapter of the Nature Conservancy in 1978, the preserve retains virtually all of its natural features, many of which have been recognized by the State's Critical Areas Program. The rough granite shoreline on the southern end of the island drops steeply off into the ocean, and the crashing waves often offer a dramatic display of the sea's strength as it batters the exposed shore.

From the parking area, you have two hiking choices: the two-mile Little Cape Point Trail and the slightly shorter Mud Hole Trail. The former bears to the right and leads you to the shore at Cape Cove and Little Cape Point. The cool, humid climate has helped create the moss-floored terrain through a mixed forest of spruce and fir, interspersed with ledges and the ubiquitous jack pine found in Maine's Down East forests. These hardy, stunted, and twisted inhabitants of thin soil have a bonsai-like appearance and cannot be found south of Maine. A unique "bog bridge" takes you through a rich swamp where pitcher plants and sundews thrive. Once at the shore, a short walk to the northeast takes you to the prominence at Little Cape Point.

The Mud Hole Trail, leaving the parking area to the left, takes you along a narrow, fjord-like cove dotted with lobster buoys and ends at Mud Hole Point with its panorama of the islands in Eastern Bay.

There are also a couple of longer hikes right along the shore, which can be a little rough in sections. One joins the Little Cape and Mud Hole Trails, and the other leads out to Red Head. Just Google Great Wass Island Preserve for an excellent map.

In addition to the scenery, the island is home to a variety of botanical rarities that cling to the bold headlands. Rarely seen elsewhere in Maine are beachhead iris, marsh felwort, and bird's-eye primrose. The bogs on Great Wass are thousands of years old, resulting from sphagnum moss that grew in basins left by retreating glaciers after the last ice age. These unique bogs are home to the rare baked-apple berry (a relative of the raspberry) and dragon's mouth orchid.

You're virtually guaranteed to see spiraling osprey and bald eagles in the sky and large rafts of common eider ducks just offshore, plus lots of other species of shorebirds abound. And what's a hike on the shore of a Maine island without seeing harbor seals sunning themselves on the warm rocks and ledges?

Be prepared, however, for fog and slippery going, which can make some of the hike difficult, or even dangerous. But with good judgment, careful planning—and good weather—your visit will be one you'll likely never forget.

Information:

www.greatwassisland.com

For a Hot Summer Hike,
Hit the Ski Slopes

M ANY OF MAINE'S SKI AREAS open their miles of trails to hikers
during the summer. Five of my favorites—Sugarloaf, Shawnee Peak, Saddleback, Sunday River, and the Camden Snow
Bowl—make for challenging hikes with unparalleled views.

Though the mechanics of hiking at a ski resort are no different than
hiking any other trail (move body up hill), it feels like a whole different
sport to me. Where a "traditional" hike puts you on a narrow wooded
path, ski trails can be the width of a football field. While most Maine hikes
feel removed from civilization, hiking at a ski resort surrounds you with
buildings and machinery.

Mountains also offer fantastically challenging hikes. Though a green
circle might seem nearly flat when you're skiing, you'd be surprised by
how steep even an easy trail is when you're hiking. Skiers look for the
most direct route when cutting trails, and a descent that follows the fall
line is never an easy ascent.

Perhaps my favorite ski area hike is an ascent of Sugarloaf in Carrabassett Valley. The climb takes you the 4,250 feet in just a few miles, making
the second-highest peak in Maine a bit easier to reach than the legendary Katahdin. From the summit, there are 360-degree views of Franklin
County and beyond, with Redington, Crocker, and Bigelow looming
large in the foreground.

Visitors are given unrestricted access to Sugarloaf's trail system, although areas where work is being done (such as this summer's new lift
installation) are occasionally blocked off. The most popular—and easiest—
route up the mountain is via Binder, the access road that runs alongside the

Tote Road ski trail. It's still a strenuous 3.5-mile hike to the summit, but the well-worn road offers hikers more tread than the surrounding slopes.

If you'd prefer a bit more wilderness in your hike, following the Appalachian Trail to Sugarloaf's summit cuts the resort's buildings and chairlifts from view.

Nearest to Portland is Shawnee Peak, a doozy of a hill with views of Bridgton and the lakes region. A ridge runs from the summit of Shawnee to the peak of Pleasant Mountain and Big Bald, and ambitious hikers can connect the mountains in a single trip. I recommend climbing the Bald Peak trail, which begins a mile south of Shawnee, and climbing down Shawnee's eastern slopes. It's a vicious ascent of nearly 1,300 feet in a bit over a mile, but Shawnee's peak is a great reward—and covered with blueberry bushes to boot.

Recently added at Shawnee Peak are the Pleasant Mountain Yurts, furnished cabins near the summit that hikers can rent. If you need something to entice you to hike, there aren't many rewards better than a comfortable bunk.

Like Sugarloaf, Saddleback is a mountain with some serious vertical and a shared summit with the Appalachian Trail. The route suggested by JoAnne Taylor, Saddleback's marketing manager, is fairly direct. Start up the main Wheeler slope from the lodge, cross over to Grey Ghost (which runs parallel to the chairlift), and then follow Tricolor up into the saddle and to the summit.

My favorite route is a long, looping run up Hudson Highway, the beginner trail that skirts the resort's western boundary. It's a much longer hike, but with a gentler slope and a great chance of seeing wildlife.

Saddleback also maintains a coffee and sandwich bar in the base lodge during the summer, open Tuesday through Saturday. Along with the much-needed nourishment, the bar has trail maps for hikers, which include routes to nearby Rock Pond, Midway Pond, and Saddleback Lake.

Saddleback's 4,121-foot peak is also accessible by the AT, via a trailhead south of Rangeley on Route 4.

With eight distinct peaks, Sunday River in Bethel offers hikers dozens of possible paths from base to summit. I recommend climbing from the South Ridge Lodge to North Peak and then following Three Mile Trail to the peaks of Barker, Locke, and White Cap. It doesn't put your feet on every part of Sunday River, but hitting five mountains out of eight isn't bad.

With 132 distinct trails, Sunday River is one of the most intimidating resorts to approach as a hiker. Luckily, Sunday River's website lists eight suggested hikes, ranging in length and difficulty. The resort has also jumped on the geocaching bandwagon, and hikers can rent GPS devices that lead them to caches of treasure on the trails.

At the Camden Snow Bowl, on Ragged Mountain, hikers are rewarded with a beautiful view of Camden Harbor and the Atlantic from the 1,300-foot peak. A view of the ocean from the hill is a bit more unique for skiers than it is for hikers, but it's a classic sight no matter the season. Along with the harbor, there are clear views of nearby hiking destinations Mount Megunticook, Maiden's Cliff, and Bald Mountain.

The quickest way up Ragged is a direct, brutal climb from the base area straight up the main slope. Clipper runs straight from the lodge to nearly the summit, and a well-worn footpath takes you the rest of the way. The hike is only about a mile each way, but you earn every single foot.

Like Sunday River and Saddleback, the Snow Bowl has a map of various hiking routes available on its website. Those looking for a longer hike can climb the mountain from a trailhead on Route 17, following a meandering route past the picturesque Mirror Lake and up the back side of Ragged.

Across the border in New Hampshire, Cannon and Loon are wonderful hikes that showcase Franconia Notch. Both also have the added benefit of lifts that run during the summer—a tram at Cannon and a gondola at Loon. Folks who hike up Loon's trails can even ride the gondola down free of charge.

The two resorts are a touch more restrictive to hikers than their Maine counterparts, so it's best to check in at the base of the lifts and see exactly where hiking is and isn't allowed.

In the high heat of summer, there's no better time to explore our state's ski resorts and think very, very cold thoughts.

Information:

www.sugarloaf.com
www.shawneepeak.com
www.saddlebackmaine.com
www.sundayriver.com
www.camdensnowbowl.com

Beautiful Bigelow

ALTHOUGH I CLIMBED BIGELOW MOUNTAIN dozens of times when I lived in the western mountains of Maine, and explored most of the terrain on the northern side of the mountain when I was involved with the group that had notions of building a mega-ski area on the broad flank above Flagstaff Lake, Columbus Day in 1984 marked a very special occasion.

It was on that day—as I reached 4,088-foot Avery Peak, one of the two spectacular cones projecting above the ridgeline on what is the last really challenging climb for through-hikers on the Appalachian Trail before they reach Mount Katahdin 180 miles to the north—that I made a vow to myself: Every year around Columbus Day, when the foliage is about at its peak, I'll climb Bigelow, not just for the sheer delight of the ascent, but as proof to myself that I still could.

And so, for the past thirty-three years, I've managed, by a variety of routes, to do it. In my mind, it is the perfect way to put an exclamation point on the end of the summer hiking season and to celebrate, once again, that I'm still alive and can.

Bigelow is a very special mountain. In the 1970s, plans to develop a ski resort were put down by Maine voters in a referendum resulting from the incredible efforts of Lance Tapley and his passionate organization, "Friends of Bigelow." The State of Maine purchased some 8,000 acres of mountainside and shorefront from the Flagstaff Corporation and patched it together with another 25,000 acres to create a very special treasure. Administered by the Bureau of Parks and Lands of the Maine Department of Conservation, this 33,000-acre parcel is called the Bigelow Mountain Preserve.

One of the things that makes Bigelow special is its sheer expanse—its Range Trail runs some 12 miles west to east from Cranberry Peak (3,194 feet) to Little Bigelow (3,025 feet). In between are the aforementioned Avery Peak, West Peak (the highest point in the range at 4,125 feet), South Horn (3,805 feet), and North Horn (3,792 feet).

Cranberry's distinctive feature is its bare ledges, and the Horns tower above little Horns Pond, stocked annually with some beautiful fish. On Avery Peak the rock foundation of the abandoned fire tower still stands.

Every few Columbus Days, if the weather's right and there's no snow on the ground, as there is about every five years, I'll commit to the twelve-mile loop up the Fire Warden's Trail from Stratton Brook Pond. It's about five miles to West Peak via Avery Peak (a word of warning: the last 1.5-mile stretch below the Bigelow Col between Avery and West Peaks rises about 1,700 vertical feet, making it one of the tougher climbs in Maine), then it's about three miles west to Horns Pond via both Horns, 2.5 miles down the Horns Pond Trail to reconnect with the Fire Warden's Trail, and then 1.6 miles back to my car at Stratton Brook Pond.

Some years I've included Little Bigelow in my hike, beginning on the Flagstaff Lake side of the mountain, and occasionally I'll begin in Stratton, climbing over Cranberry Peak past Cranberry Pond and down the Appalachian Trail heading south, but this requires two cars and a couple of people so you can shuttle back up to Stratton.

The shortest way to Avery Peak, and the easiest I've found over many years of ascents, is via the Safford Brook Trail from the north up through Safford Notch, around the breathtaking Old Man's Head (with its commanding view down the Carrabassett River), and along a bold section of ridge to the peak. This route covers some 4.2 miles each way, and it has become my route of choice about every third year. If there's snow on the ground, I encourage you to opt for this route, as the scramble up the last mile over snow-covered rocks on the Fire Warden's Trail can be a killer.

Another thing that distinguishes the Safford Brook route is that you'll be following what was Amos Winter's original ski trail that he cut in the late 1940s with a bunch of Kingfield locals who became known as The Bigelow Boys. They widened sections of the Appalachian Trail and the old Shingle Mill Trail running down to the Dead River, giving themselves a place to ski without having to go all the way to Tuckerman Ravine on Mount Washington. When Central Maine Power Company built Long Falls Dam to form Flagstaff Lake, Amos and the Boys turned their attention to the next 4,000-footer to the south—Sugarloaf—and the rest, as they say, is history.

Every few years I'm treated to one of nature's great juxtapositions as I sit at the summit, drinking in the view of Sugarloaf to the south and thanking God (and Lance Tapley) for this truly remarkable treasure, and for the fact I'm still able to enjoy it. On those years, the contrast between the crimson, yellow, and green foliage with the snow cover on Sugarloaf's peak and the still bright green fairways of the golf course at the base of the mountain is almost more than my mind can process.

Map: www.mainehuts.org/wp-content/uploads/bigelowmap3.pdf

Hidden in the Hundred Mile Wilderness

A STATE WITH A RICH PAST OF INDUSTRY in its wilderness, Maine has a number of spots that offer a mix of history and outdoor adventure. One such example is the remains of Katahdin Iron Works, which borders some of the state's most stunning natural features.

A few miles north of Brownville Junction on Route 11, signs direct visitors to the Katahdin Iron Works Historic Site. Though all that remains are a restored blast furnace and a "beehive" charcoal kiln, this used to be the largest iron operation in the state.

In the mid–1800s, iron ore was found in nearby Ore Mountain. In 1843, the blast furnace was built, and over the years the operation ballooned. It's hard to believe when you visit now, but in 1884 there was a company town here with more than 200 homes. In 1890, outside competition forced the iron works to shut down. Many people left town after that, also leaving a floundering spool mill.

The land containing the kiln and furnace was eventually donated to the state in 1968, and is now managed by the Bureau of Parks and Lands. Plaques and informative brochures at the site paint a more detailed picture of its unique history. There's also a fascinating look at the entire ore-processing line, from raw material to iron bars.

Like Maine's many other historical sites, the remains of the Katahdin Iron Works are worthy of a trip on their own. But it would be a mistake to not mention the stunning attractions around the site.

Just north of the iron works, the Hermitage and Gulf Hagas greet curious visitors. As long as the road to reach them is passable, you can continue past the historical site to the trailhead. A day-use fee of $4 includes a map from Diamond Corporation, which manages the land.

Seven miles north of the iron works, there's a parking area for the Appalachian Trail. The trail to Gulf Hagas is shared with the AT for about a mile, then the Appalachian heads east for White Cap and the Hagas trail continues north.

The trail travels parallel to a stream for 0.7 miles, before a ford of the Pleasant River. About a mile into the hike, you enter the Hermitage, a stand of massive old-growth white pines. Spreading across thirty-five acres and protected by the Maine Chapter of the Nature Conservancy, the Hermitage is recognized as a National Natural Landmark. If Gulf Hagas is the Grand Canyon of Maine, the Hermitage is our redwood forest—some of the pines are more than 130 feet tall.

Soon after the Hermitage, you'll see Screw Auger, the first of Hagas's many waterfalls. A skinny four-foot-wide fall, the water cascades twenty-six feet into the canyon. Only a few minutes farther down the trail is Hammond Street pitch, a ninety-foot cliff that looks down at the gorge below.

Next stop is the Jaws, a wide, surging stretch of water. Formerly a narrow channel, its canyon walls were blown open with dynamite by log drivers around the turn of the twentieth century. Looking at the water rushing through to Gulf Hagas, it's hard to believe that log drives used to run through the canyon.

Less than half a mile farther along the rim is Buttermilk Falls. The name makes sense—the falls churn up froth, and the milky water doesn't look far from its namesake. Just ahead on the trail are Billings and Stairs Falls, further upping your waterfall tally.

Next is the Head of the Gulf, where an island bisects the river into two impressive falls.

At this point you're about four miles in, and it's a good spot to rest before completing your circuit and heading back to your car.

If you've got an extra vehicle, you can leave a car by Lloyd Pond, only a mile above the Head. Otherwise, it's back through the woods to the Hermitage and your vehicle.

I should note that, while the Gulf Hagas trail is a hike that can be done in a single day, it isn't an easy one. The hike is a ten-mile circuit coming from the Appalachian Trail lot and includes a stream ford and lots of rugged, rocky terrain. The main trail has plenty of spurs, which lead to some great viewpoints but add mileage to the hike.

The description of Gulf Hagas as a mini-Grand Canyon is apt, and there are some gut-churningly steep drops where the trail follows the edge of the gorge.

As you should for any hike, be prepared and don't go alone, if for no other reason than the fact that there are so many memorable scenes along the way that you'll want to share the experience.

Hidden in the Hundred Mile Wilderness, Katahdin Iron Works, the Hermitage, and Gulf Hagas are worth the long trip to reach them. There's plenty of history and adventure there to fill a Maine summer day.

Hiking (and Fishing) Snow Mountain

NOT FAR FROM THE CANADIAN BORDER on Route 27, just below Sarampus Falls on the Dead River in Alder Stream Township, and south of the beautiful Chain of Ponds leading to the frontier, there's a road to the west leading into part of the Penobscot Indian Territory.

Identified by a sign explaining the rules that apply in the area, the road is about seventeen miles north of the intersection of Routes 16 and 27 in Stratton. It leads to a favorite hike of mine, with an added bonus if you happen to like to cast a fly. Snow Mountain, only fifty-two feet shy of joining Maine's fourteen elite four-thousand footers, is a hike overlooked by many. But it's a must if you want to see an extended sweep of the western mountains, a stretch of Benedict Arnold's route to Quebec in 1775 along the headwaters of the Dead River, and views of Canada all the way to Lac Megantic.

There's a chance that the gate at Route 27 may be locked, which will extend your round-trip hike by about ten miles, but over the many years I've been going there, the gate has always been open. If that's the case, you'll follow a well-maintained gravel road for 3.9 miles, take a right at the fork, and proceed 1.1 miles to a parking lot and the Snow Mountain trailhead. If you want to camp, you must obtain a permit from the Penobscot Indian Nation Department of Trust Responsibilities:

Penobscot Indian Nation
Tribal Administration
12 Wabanaki Way
Indian Island, ME 04468

Telephone: (207) 827-7776
Fax: (207) 817-7482

The trail consists of old logging roads, and has recently been relocated in spots to protect wildlife and fish habitat. After about two miles, a spur heads left to Snow Mountain Pond and the former fire warden's camp, which is now private property. Leaving the pond, the trail climbs steeply north, past a welcome freshwater spring. Near the summit, it connects with a trail to the left that leads to Big Island Pond. Shortly after, there's a great viewpoint back to the south.

At the summit, a climb of 1.3 miles from the pond, the remains of the old fire tower still stand. Clambering up it will give you fabulous 360-degree views of the surrounding wilderness. There's a great view of the parade of wind power turbines on the flanks of neighboring Kibby Mountain.

The bonus of a trip up Snow Mountain is, for me, the chance on the way back to cast a fly in Snow Mountain Pond. And on one trip, I had such fun fishing there on the way up that I never made it to the summit. Speaking of that trip, I owe a special debt of gratitude to the owner of the old overturned aluminum skiff that I commandeered for fishing—it's tough to find a spot to fish from the shore on the entire perimeter of the pond. Thank you, whoever you are—I promise I left it in the same condition I found it.

You can complete a great day in Franklin County if you bring along your kayak and pop it into Flagstaff Lake on your way home. The public boat launch is on Route 27 just north of Stratton where the South Branch of the Dead River passes under a bridge.

You can paddle out into the lake and explore the North Branch of the Dead River up toward Cathedral Pines in Eustis, or down toward the village of Stratton. One of your rewards is a spectacular view of the Bigelow Range.

I like to head up the South Branch, and in early summer you can go upstream for a couple of miles. There are some sandbars that make for perfect lunch spots, and at least three sets of rapids that you can work your way up before turning around and scooting back down for a bit of an easy whitewater thrill.

If you go later in the summer, there's a good chance the river will be low and you'll need to turn back after only a mile or so. Still, it's nonetheless a great paddle.

The Borestone Mountain
Audubon Sanctuary
The Perfect Fall Hike

TUCKED AWAY IN ELLIOTSVILLE PLANTATION, some ten miles northeast of Monson, a special treasure awaits nature lovers and hikers, especially on a cool fall day when Mother Nature has worked her magic on the hardwoods and the brilliant hues of fall adorn the countryside.

The Borestone Mountain Audubon Sanctuary, developed, owned, and operated by Maine Audubon, comprises more than 1,600 acres of northern hardwood and boreal forest that has been uncut for over a century, three small ponds, and two craggy summits just south of the Appalachian Trail and Maine's Northern Forest.

Originally operated as a fox farm in the early 1900s, the property was bequeathed to the National Audubon Society by its owner, ornithologist Robert T. Moore. Gifts by his son and daughter, as well as other generous donors, enlarged the original acreage to its present size.

I discovered the sanctuary several years ago on a trip to climb Barren Mountain on the AT as a continuation of my now-completed effort to summit every mountain in Maine near or over three thousand feet in elevation. Barren is the highest (nearly 2,700 feet) and most accessible mountain of the Barren-Chairback Range. It happens that the access road to the Barren trailhead passes the parking area for the sanctuary, and I learned about it from an information board at the sanctuary gate, which opens at 8 a.m. daily from Memorial Day through October 31.

I have fine-tuned my summer hiking schedule over the years to annually include some undiscovered mountain or two, which now requires a bushwhack, as I don't think there's a mountain of any size in Maine with a trail that I haven't bagged—a reference to the peak-bagging tradition among hikers. Another tradition is to revisit my favorite hikes, whether in the mountains or Down East, where the Cobscook Trails around Cob-scook Bay and the Bold Coast region beckon irresistibly. Borestone falls in the latter category, and I often climb it early in the summer and then again in early October to enjoy the foliage gaudily on display there.

The trailhead is at about 800 feet above sea level, so the entire three-mile hike to the 2,000-foot East Peak involves an ascent of only 1,200 feet. The first mile and a third climbs five hundred feet to a seasonally-staffed visitors center perched on the shore of tiny Sunrise Pond. Don't make the mistake of hauling your fly rod, as I did on my first trip, as there's no fishing allowed—in fact, I'm told there are no fish in any of the three con-nected ponds, which include, east to west, Sunrise, Midday, and Sunset. Not only is fishing not allowed, neither are pets, fires, hunting, firearms, trapping, collecting, off-road vehicles, camping, or alcoholic beverages—the pristine Maine woods at their best.

At the visitors center you'll find wildlife and natural exhibits, help-ful staff, and even a composting toilet. A modest fee is collected from non-Audubon members (adults $4, seniors/students/school and nonprofit groups $2, children under six free).

Leaving the center, you'll proceed around the southeastern end of Sunrise Pond, cross the outlet, and then ascend rather steeply for about a mile to the open rocks of West Peak. There you'll drink in the vista. To the north you'll see Barren Mountain and pristine Onawa Lake, and Sebec Lake to the south. A short hike down through a saddle will take you to West Peak, another open summit with unobstructed 360-degree views.

I'm continually amazed when I talk with fellow explorers of Maine's outdoor treasures how many of them have yet to get to Borestone. It's on my short list of must-see destinations. And I suggest that it be on yours.

As if Borestone isn't enough of a reason to head off the beaten path in Monson, a special treat awaits you on a trail that starts a short distance up Little Wilson Stream, which you cross just before the Borestone park-ing lot. It's Little Wilson Falls, a fifty-seven-foot waterfall gouged by the stream through slate, a prevalent local mineral. The hike is about a mile and a half, and you'll find the falls a short distance after you've connected with the AT, just before a small pond.

Map, pics, and so forth: www.maineaudubon.org

Check the Appalachian Mountain Club's *Maine Mountain Guide,* my hik-ing bible, for definitive directions . . . not only for this hike but virtually any mountain ascent in Maine.

Ladder Hikes Are a Step Up in Acadia

THE AREA THAT IS NOW ACADIA NATIONAL PARK has been a haven for visitors for centuries, starting with French explorers in the early 1600s. In the twentieth century the park progressed from Sieur de Monts National Monument (1916) to Lafayette National Park (1919) to Acadia National Park in 1929. Acadia now spans an impressive 47,000 acres, with most on Mount Desert Island. The park is one of the most popular in the national park system and draws more than two million visitors each year.

This huge volume of visitors is the reason that I—along with many other Mainers—tend to avoid Acadia during the summer. The bulk of the tourists visit in July, August, and September, and MDI's scenic two-lane roads begin to look like the Los Angeles freeway. It's great for the town and the park, sure, but it makes solitude-seeking adventurers feel claustrophobic. But sometimes Acadia's 100-plus miles of hiking trails are worth the trip, even if it means navigating crowds of flatlanders.

My favorite way to experience Acadian hiking is via the park's four "ladder" trails: Beech Cliff, Beehive, Penobscot, and Precipice. These unique trails combine traditional hiking with climbs on ladders, rungs drilled into rock faces, and metal bars used for balance and assistance. The near-vertical climb of these trails makes for good exercise, and hikers can cover loads of vertical in a short time.

The Beech Cliff Trail climbs from the parking lot at Echo Lake, transitioning quickly from flat ground to stone steps to iron ladders. An open summit, reached after less than a mile, provides stellar views of Acadia and Sergeant Mountains, Somes Sound, and Great Cranberry Island. A hike south from the summit gives a gentler route back to Echo Lake Beach Road (and your vehicle), making for a round-trip that's only about two miles.

Beehive Mountain, which towers to the west of the park's loop road, is one of Acadia's most popular hikes. Ascending from the Sand Beach parking area and up ladders and along ledges, the 0.8-mile trail climbs over 500 feet to the summit. The trail can get quite crowded (I suggest hitting it before 10 a.m. or after 4 p.m.), and on busy days tourists at the nearby Sand Beach get a colorful view of hikers swarming the mountain like ants. A cool alpine pond, termed The Bowl, sits just beyond the summit—a great reward for hikers who make the climb. The Bowl Trail skirts past the pond and wraps back down to the trailhead.

The longest hike on this list, the trail up Penobscot Mountain, showcases the area around Acadia's Jordan Pond. There are multiple routes to Penobscot's 1,194-foot summit; I recommend the Jordan Cliffs trail, which rises from the Jordan Pond House parking lot and features a mix of stone and timber box steps, iron rungs, railings, and bridges. The exposed route follows a cliff band looking down on Jordan for more than a mile, making for fun (if slightly harrowing) hiking. A quick half-mile spur at the end takes hikers to the summit of Penobscot. The Penobscot Mountain Trail leads visitors down a less-exposed route back to the trailhead. Enjoy the four-mile hike and treat yourself to a snack at the locally run Jordan Pond House restaurant after you finish.

Acadia's most famous trail, The Precipice, takes hikers straight up the east face of Champlain Mountain. While it isn't technical climbing, the sheer drops and strenuous climb will certainly test the mettle of many. The 0.9-mile ascent starts from a parking area off the loop road, and almost immediately starts its dramatic climb along open ledges and over 100-foot drops. The Precipice Trail isn't fooling around—don't hike the trail if you aren't an experienced hiker, if you're afraid of heights, or if it's wet. Plenty of other trails, like the Beachcroft Trail (on Route 3) and the Champlain South Ridge Trail (from Beehive's summit), provide less harrowing access to Champlain's scenic 1,058-foot summit.

Also, check the status of Precipice before you plan your trip. It's one of a handful of Acadia's trails that the park closes for nesting peregrine falcons. The National Park Service's Acadia website (nps.gov/acad) provides up-to-date listings of trail closures.

While I still prefer the solitude and cool temperatures of the spring and fall on Mount Desert Island, this was a great reminder that it's sometimes worth fighting the crowds. Acadia undoubtedly shines during the summer, and there's no better way to experience it than the dramatic ladder hikes.

Gilsland Farm
A Gem Hidden in Plain Sight

BLINK AS YOU'RE HEADED NORTH ON ROUTE 1 into Falmouth and you might miss the entrance to Maine Audubon's Gilsland Farm Center. I'd suggest keeping your eyes open and turning into the Maine Audubon's headquarters, a sixty-five-acre outdoor playground for nature lovers—all just minutes from the center of Portland.

While Maine Audubon's headquarters has been located at Gilsland Farm since the 1970s, the land has a history stretching back thousands of years. Ages before the first English settlers arrived in Maine in the 1600s, the Wabanakis took advantage of the spot. The combination of tidal flats, the Presumpscot River, and a relatively calm part of Casco Bay made for an ideal settling place. Once the English arrived, they split the land up and cleared timber to create farms and harvest timber, hence the large meadows that make up much of the sanctuary today.

Today, the land is home to the Gilsland Farm Audubon Center, an environmentally friendly building that houses offices, facilities for public programming, a Maine Audubon Nature Store and the Teacher's Resource Center.

It's also home to nearly three miles of hiking trails that show off the diversity of the land that borders Casco Bay and the Presumpscot. It isn't a terribly strenuous set of hiking trails—you can easily walk the entire network in a morning—but the flora and fauna are impressive.

The shortest and easiest trail on the grounds is the Pond Meadow Trail, a half-mile jaunt that takes you (nearly literally) over the river and through the woods. The visitor's guide promises that the trail offers the "greatest diversity of habitat on the sanctuary," as it leads visitors alongside a pond, through oak and hemlock woods, and to marshes on the Presumpscot Estuary.

The West Meadow Trail offers the best views of Portland, winding through an open meadow to bluffs looking toward the Forest City. The trail also leads to two of the sanctuary's three observation blinds, so if you're a birder, you'll find secluded spots to park with binoculars.

Where the other trails have spurs and paths winding through them, the North Meadow Trail is a long loop around the northern end of the property. In my experience, the trail has also been the best place to spot wildlife at Gilsland. Fox and deer definitely prowl through the meadows early in the morning, and there are a large number of woodchucks on the grounds. Bird lovers will also find a third observation blind and an osprey platform on the North Meadow Trail.

The trails at Gilsland Farm aren't taxing, but that's a nice reminder that every hike doesn't need to be an extreme workout. I won't abandon the Precipice Trail or Goose Eye Mountain anytime soon, but it's great to have such a diverse habitat in Portland's backyard. Not only that, but the trails at the Audubon sanctuary are pleasantly family- and kid-friendly.

Along with its network of trails, there are plenty of programs and classes at Gilsland Farm. Some, like a Thursday morning bird-watching hike, are weekly affairs. Others are one-off talks or events. Full event listings can be found on the Maine Audubon website (maineaudubon.com). Events can be attended by the public and Maine Audubon members, with prices for members usually significantly slashed.

I've talked with a number of people on the peninsula who, despite our proximity, have never made it out to Gilsland Farm. If you're used to the Portland Trails network and want a change of scenery that can make you forget you're right next to the city, the Gilsland Farm Center is an oasis of Maine's natural beauty.

Hiking on Campobello

AMPOBELLO IS TECHNICALLY NOT IN MAINE, and a passport is required to cross the bridge over the Lubec Narrows from the United States to get to this special New Brunswick, Canada, island. It has become a tradition for our family to visit for a few days every summer to hike the myriad scenic trails.

The easiest way to get to the island is the Franklin Delano Roosevelt Bridge from Lubec. It's only about ten miles down Route 189 after leaving Whiting on Route 1 some fifteen miles east of Machias.

Another route to the island includes a couple of ferry rides of less than a half hour, and I highly recommend this option for your trip either to or from the island. Slightly farther for most Mainers, this alternative begins in the small New Brunswick town of L'Etete, about a half hour east of the border crossing in Calais, and a short drive down a peninsula from historic St. George. A free ferry runs sixteen hours a day to and from Deer Island. You'll drive the twelve-mile length of Deer Island to pick up another ferry to Wilson's Beach on Campobello. This ferry leaves every hour on the half hour and runs from late June to mid-September ten hours a day.

Whichever way you take, you'll end up in another country and, from the hiker's perspective, another world, as the alternatives in both the International Park and the abutting Herring Cove Provincial Park offer a wide variety of options, all easy enough for the casual weekend hiker, but varied enough for inveterate outdoor enthusiasts.

The International Park comprises nearly 3,000 acres, and Herring Cove Park nearly half as many again. The seaside perimeter of the former offers more than ten miles of spectacular scenery, and Herring Cove Park features several more miles of both oceanfront and forested hiking.

In the International Park, the trails wind through and past natural habitats forested with spruce and fir and a variety of hardwoods, as well as sphagnum bogs, fields, and seashore. Hikes can be planned for some of the shorter trails or, in combination, moderate to long excursions. Several of the trails include observation areas and decks overlooking steep cliffs and ledges. Needless to say, caution is advised near the overlooks. Coastal weather conditions and algae and moss may make some of the trails, observation decks, and footbridges slippery, so be sure to wear your hiking boots. Watch the tides if you're planning a perimeter hike, as some portions of the trails that pass around points extending into the bay are covered at high tide.

Two short trails that are not connected to the perimeter trail are worth visiting—one for the view and the other for a lesson in natural history. The former is a relatively easy hike from the Park Visitor Center to Friar's Head. It's only a little more than half a mile and ends at an observation deck overlooking Lubec to the west. It's a great spot to sight seals and the occasional whale. On one visit, I kayaked in the shadow of the head around some salmon pens that were also appealing to a large number of seals circling them.

The other short hike, also about half a mile, follows a wooden pathway through Eagle Hill Bog, where interpretive panels explain the variety of flora and fauna. Masses of leatherleaf, sheep laurel, pale laurel, and bog rosemary abound as well as interesting shrubs that grow among the mosses. Beaver ponds add to the scenic variety on this short trail.

Your long hiking adventure starts at the Campobello Island Tourist Information Center shortly after crossing the bridge on Route 774. The trail passes around Deep Cove, out around Cranberry Point, skirts two small bays known as the Upper and Lower Duck Ponds (aptly named for the large numbers of ducks gathered there), and leads to Liberty Point, the southernmost tip of the island. From there, views of Grand Manan to the west are enhanced by the presence of seals basking on Sugar Loaf Rock.

Turning north along the shore, the trail leads for about two and a half miles to Raccoon Beach and past Ragged Point with its striking SunSweep sculpture, carved from a slab of Canadian black granite. It is a part of an international art project that includes similar sculptures in Minnesota and Washington State.

From Raccoon Beach it's a short walk on a gravel road to link up with the Gibraltar Rock Trail leading through the provincial park to beautiful and uncrowded mile-long Herring Cove Beach.

If you're not into hiking, Campobello Sightseeing has a van that leaves the Roosevelt Park Visitor Center at 10:30 a.m. and 2 p.m. daily from June 15 until September 15. The van takes up to fifteen people on informative and interesting two-and-a-half-hour tours of the island.

Information:

www.visitcampobello.com

Jewell Falls
A Special Place in the Fore River Sanctuary

D ID YOU KNOW THAT PORTLAND IS HOME to a natural thirty-foot waterfall? Located in the eighty-five-acre Fore River Sanctuary, Jewell Falls is just a short hike from a number of Portland's major thoroughfares. The falls are named after Portland Trails cofounder Tom Jewell, who donated the tract of land that comprises the sanctuary to the organization. It isn't the most impressive falls in the state—Jewell is downright puny compared to Angel and Moxie Falls—but it's certainly not something you'd expect to find just a few minutes from Congress Street.

There are four entrances to the Fore River Sanctuary, so it's easy to reach Jewell Falls or any of the other attractions within. Parking at Maine Orthopedics on Frost Street puts you just moments from the southernmost trailhead. This entrance follows an old canal towpath, a visible relic of a former shipping route.

Parking lots at the ends of Rowe Avenue and Starbird Lane provide access to the western and eastern entrances of the sanctuary, respectively. A fourth trailhead, at the end of Hillcrest Avenue, provides the easiest access to visitors who wish to see Jewell Falls without much of a hike. From this northern entrance, it's only a few hundred feet from the parking lot to the waterfall.

Coming from the north, you first reach a wooden bridge that spans the water above the falls. A path runs alongside the falls to a small clearing at the bottom, where there's a stone bench dedicated to Jewell. The water doesn't fall in a single cascade, but over a number of small steps before continuing toward Portland Harbor. The myriad streams running down the rocks make for a waterfall that's visually interesting. Though it won't be mistaken for Niagara, in the spring or after heavy rain, the water flows a bit more vigorously.

Despite the heavy traffic the spot certainly gets, it's meticulously maintained. Every time I've visited, the area—and the entire sanctuary—has been clean and clear of rubbish.

The waterfall isn't the only attraction for Fore River Sanctuary visitors, though it is likely the largest draw. The marshland where the river meets the ocean is popular with bird-watchers, and the entirety of the preserve is open to mountain bikers. The site, open daily from dawn until dusk, also connects to the larger Portland Trails network.

The flowing waters of the sanctuary occupy an interesting place in Portland's history as a piece of the former Cumberland and Oxford Canal. In the 1830s, a canal ran from the lakes region to Portland Harbor, following the Presumpscot River before diverging toward the Fore River (and through the Fore River Sanctuary) and into the harbor. Despite the scenic path, the canal wasn't there for tourists. In the days before railroads crisscrossed Maine, the canal was an important shipping route for everything from apples to gunpowder.

Shortly after the Civil War, different modes of transport usurped the canal. Over a century later, you can still see the remains of the former shipping channel in the sanctuary and elsewhere between Portland and Harrison.

The sanctuary is just one reminder of the great work Portland Trails has done not just creating walking path and trails, but protecting land and water from the growing city. Now in its twenty-first year, the nonprofit land trust maintains fifty miles of trails in Portland and surrounding towns. It's hard to count the number of hours I've spent on the trails over the last few years, though they surely figure in the hundreds. If you've ever driven by the Back Cove on a beautiful day, you know just how many people enjoy their most popular trail.

Despite my lighthearted introduction, Jewell Falls are far from trivial. The waterfall, the surrounding sanctuary, and the entire network of Portland Trails are reminders of the intersection of the natural and the developed that occurs so frequently in Maine. In cities large or small, residents aren't often lucky enough to have a waterfall literally in their backyard.

Plenty to Please Near Damariscotta River

To the uninitiated, the Damariscotta River region might seem like a bust for hikers. It's a pretty area, for sure, but the rolling coastal hills don't scream "hike here." It would, however, be a shame to skip the region based on this first impression, as there's plenty of spots for day hikers to explore.

On both sides of the Damariscotta River, there are great spots for outdoor enthusiasts to spend a few hours. On the east bank of the river, the remains of the famous Whaleback Shell Midden greets curious explorers. On the west side, trails at Glidden Point and Dodge Point offer more serious hiking.

Located just north of Damariscotta on Route 1, the Whaleback Shell Midden is one of Maine's oldest man-made attractions. The midden is a massive construction of oyster shells built over a millennium ago. Shell middens are enormous heaps of oyster shells built by coastal Native Americans. The Whaleback Midden in Damariscotta (named for its distinctive shape) was built by the Abenaki and Algonquin people that lived in the area before European colonists arrived.

While they're interesting to look at, in reality they're little more than very old garbage piles. Ancient peoples deposited oyster shells in heaps along the coast, along with other detritus such as pots, tools, and bones. The molecular makeup of oyster shells made the surrounding soil much less acidic, so instead of breaking down, these middens have remained for centuries. Over the years, they got larger and larger, creating an all-natural time capsule. Though there are shell middens all along the coast of America—and, indeed, coastal regions around the world—the ones in Damariscotta are among the largest.

The trail to the midden is a scenic loop that takes visitors through an apple orchard and along the shore of the Damariscotta River. At only half a mile in length, the trail is an easy hike regardless of fitness level. Just beyond the head of the trail is an overlook offering views of the Great Salt Bay.

Down the river from the Whaleback Midden is Glidden Point and the Salt Bay Heritage Trail. With a trailhead on Route 215 in Newcastle, the three-mile loop is only minutes away from the Whaleback site. The gentle trail runs the gamut of coastal environments, taking hikers through marshland, forests, coastline, pastures, and even an old sheep tunnel. A side trail provides access to Glidden Point's own ancient shell middens.

A bit farther down the Boothbay Peninsula, the Dodge Point Public Reserved Land boasts 521 acres of public land, 8,000 feet of shoreline and beaches, and a trail network with six miles of hiking terrain. The four paths—the challenging 1.2-mile Ravine Trail, the waterfront 1.5-mile Shore Trail, and the gentle two-mile Old Farm Road Trail and 0.8-mile Timber Trail—give hikers myriad options.

The trailhead for the Dodge Point trails is three miles south of downtown Damariscotta on River Road, and a map of all four trails is available at a kiosk in the parking area.

Much of the credit for the trails around Damariscotta goes to the Damariscotta River Association, a nonprofit group that protects and manages more than 2,900 acres of land and twenty-two miles of fresh- and saltwater shoreline in the area. The Glidden, Dodge, and Whaleback sites are all managed either wholly or partially by the DRA.

The Damariscotta River Association covers far more trails and lands than the few mentioned here, and more information and maps can be found at the DRA headquarters in Damariscotta. The Salt Bay Farm Heritage Center is located at 110 Belvedere Road, and is open 9 a.m. to 5 p.m. on weekdays. It's an outdoor attraction itself, with a mile of shorefront and swaths of field and marshland.

For the ambitious, it's possible to hike from Dodge Point down to McKay Road in Edgecomb, a five-mile trip each way. The route is part of the River-Link project, a joint effort by a number of land trusts and property owners to create a continuous recreational corridor between the Damariscotta and Sheepscot Rivers. The project began in 2006 and will grow to include even more terrain.

Not every hike needs to be a mettle-testing ordeal with slopes and double-digit mileage. Sometimes, it's nice to relax and take in Maine's beautiful scenery and rich history. The trails in the Damariscotta River region allow hikers to escape the crush of tourists just miles away and disappear into a different time, whether it's farmlands that are hundreds of years old or middens that are thousands.

Rangeley's Range of Outdoor Activities

L EGENDARY SKIING, SNOWMOBILE TRAILS, AND ICE FISHING have long attracted visitors to Rangeley in the winter. When so much of the marketing of Maine focuses tourists on the coast during the summer and fall, it's easy to forget that the interior of the state is a four-season playground.

The easiest way to reach Rangeley is to follow Route 4 from Farmington. The scenic forty-mile drive takes less than an hour, as long as the weather is good, and many stretches of the road have been rehabbed in recent years.

If you're traveling alone, bring some music to keep you company—once you pass through Strong, a radio signal is tough to find.

Routes 16 and 17 make for longer trips into the Rangeley Lakes region, but they aren't without their charm. Taking Route 17 from Rumford affords spectacular views of Mooselookmeguntic and New Hampshire from Height of Land, and a drive on Route 16 means traveling through Carrabassett Valley past Sugarloaf and Bigelow.

From downtown Rangeley, you're just a few miles from day hikes, no matter which direction you go.

About nine miles south of Rangeley on Route 4, you'll find access to the summit of 4,120-foot Saddleback, via the Appalachian Trail. At just over five miles, the hike to the peak is about twice as long as going up the ski slopes, but offers a much more gradual climb.

The Appalachian Trail route also passes Piazza Rock, a formation that appears to be suspended in midair, less than two miles from the Route 4 parking area. It's a flat, easy hike that's perfect for kids and casual hikers.

Easy trails on the north and south shores of Rangeley Lake provide water access for hikers. On the north side, the Hunter Cove Wildlife Sanctuary has 1.5 miles of trails with access to the cove. To the south, the 869-acre Rangeley Lake State Park is home to campsites, hiking trails, and a picnic area.

Angel Falls, a ninety-foot tiered waterfall less than thirty miles from downtown Rangeley, is one of Maine's most scenic places. A quick trip south on Route 17 from Rangeley, followed by a few miles on Houghton and Bemis Roads, leads to a small parking area.

If you're searching for Angel Falls, a GPS system or a copy of the *Maine Atlas and Gazetteer* is highly recommended. The falls are easy to miss, and Houghton and Bemis are both logging roads without clearly marked mileages.

The hike to the waterfall is short—less than a mile each way—but involves a number of river fords that require sure-footedness to stay dry.

The Rangeley area also has loads of options for cyclists and kayakers.

The Railroad Bike Loop Trail, which starts on Depot Street in Rangeley, covers a dozen miles of mixed terrain. The trail takes bikers past Haley Pond, Gull Pond, and Saddleback Lake on state roads, double-track roads, and old railroad beds before following Dallas Hill Road and Route 4 back to town.

The East Kennebago Mountain Trail, ten miles east of Rangeley on Route 16, is noted by folks at the Sugarloaf and Saddleback resorts as an ideal mountain-biking trail. The six-mile (round-trip) trail has some stellar views of several of Maine's 4,000-plus-footers—Redington, Sugarloaf, Spaulding, and Abraham.

For kayaks and canoes, the easiest place to get on the water is the free boat launch area at Lakeside Park on Main Street. Coves and islands dot the ten-square-mile lake, and there's more to explore than you'll see in a single day.

A number of Rangeley's lakeside shops offer canoe and kayak rentals, and some offer guided tours. Some local outfitters for nearby river trips offer shuttle service to put-in points.

For the truly ambitious paddler, the Rangeley Lakes are but a single piece of the 740-mile Northern Forest Canoe Trail, a paddling route that runs from Fort Kent to Old Forge, New York. The trail was completed in 2006, and the organizers' website (northernforestcanoetrail.org) offers itineraries for doing the trail in part or in full.

I should also mention the fish in the Rangeley region's many lakes and streams. A strong commitment to sustainable fishing and catch-and-release programs has bred a world-famous population of landlocked salmon and brook trout.

Something for Everyone on Tumbledown

A BONUS ABOUT HIKING IN MAINE is that the state offers so many different things to so many people. Many of Maine's hikes allow access to dramatic cliff faces, alpine ponds, bald ridges, and closely clustered peaks. One reason that Weld's Tumbledown Mountain is my favorite hike in the state is because it offers all these features in one place.

Tumbledown consists of three distinct peaks that ring an alpine pond, colloquially called Crater Lake or Tumbledown Pond. The East and West Peaks are accessible by well-traveled trails, and the North Peak can be reached with a bit of bushwhacking. Three distinct trails—the Brook, Parker Ridge, and Loop Trails—all climb to Tumbledown Pond. The pond serves triple-duty as a good lunch spot, a clear camping spot, and a common point of departure to all three peaks.

Though the routes up Tumbledown are steep enough to provide a challenge, I've always found the most vexing part of the hikes to be finding the trailheads. Before heading to Tumbledown, remember that a *DeLorme Gazetteer*, a GPS, and a functioning odometer are your friends.

Coming from southern or central Maine, make your way to the intersection of Routes 4 and 156 in Wilton. Follow 156 into Weld, continuing straight through Weld Village. Just beyond the village, take a left at a big sign for Webb Corner—this is where you want to reset your odometer. You hit a dirt road called Byron Road after a few hundred yards. The Brook Trail leaves Byron Road 4.4 miles from Webb Corner, and the Loop Trail leaves Byron Road 5.8 miles from the turn.

My favorite route up Tumbledown is the Brook Trail. It's a short and sweet hike to the pond, fairly steep but not too strenuous. The trail leaves from a large parking lot (complete with outhouse) on Byron Road and follows an old, flat logging road for its first mile. At the one-mile mark, you head into the woods and start a more dramatic ascent. The rocky trail more or less follows a brook flowing down from Tumbledown Pond. After a mile and a half of climbing and switchbacks, the trail reaches the pond.

In years past, the Parker Ridge Trail was accessed from a trailhead on the privately owned Morgan Road. I don't want to encourage you to trespass on private property, so I suggest accessing Parker Ridge from the Brook Trail. Just beyond the Brook trailhead, a trail called the Little Jackson Connector heads off to the right. After about a mile, a turn to the left will put you on the old Parker Ridge Trail, while bearing right will take you toward the summit of Little Jackson. Like the Brook Trail, Parker Ridge climbs at a gentle slope for about a mile before getting significantly steeper. The trail takes hikers up to the bare summit of Parker Ridge, which sits above Tumbledown Pond, before descending to connect with the Brook Trail at the alpine pond.

The Loop Trail leaves from a trailhead about a mile and a half up the road from the Brook Trail. Again, the trail is fairly flat for the first mile. The transition to a steeper climb is marked by a large boulder, appropriately called Tumbledown Boulder. The Loop Trail is a bit more exposed than the trails leaving from the Brook trailhead, which makes for nice views but also means a lot more scrambling over rocks and boulders. After crossing a brook, the trail continues through a gully to a tight fissure, where iron rungs provide help for the rest of the ascent. It's because of this tight passage—called Fat Man's Misery—that hiking the Loop Trail with kids, dogs, or a large pack isn't recommended. After struggling through the tight squeeze, it's only a few hundred yards to Tumbledown Pond.

All three trails lead to Tumbledown Pond, which is destination enough for most hikers. Bare ground on the shores provides popular spots for travelers with tents, and if you hike early enough, you're likely to see campers taking a morning swim. The pond is also a haven for fishermen, and you may encounter folks headed down the trail with their day's catch.

If you'd like to reach the summits surrounding the water, the short Tumbledown Ridge trail connects the East and West Peaks. It's only about a mile from one to the other, so if you're planning on bagging peaks, it's worth the effort to hit both. The North Peak is a bit harder to reach, as there's no maintained trail to the summit. The easiest route is from the East Peak, where you can hack your way through the saddle separating the peaks up to its summit.

All the routes up Tumbledown are short and easily manageable day hikes, and they're well worth the effort to visit the mountain's unique features. Just don't forget to bring your *Gazetteer*.

Get a Look at Fall's Finery

ROM OUR ROUGH, ROCKY COAST to mountains and waterfalls farther inland, Maine possesses some of the most stunning foliage spots in the United States. And autumn brings a steady stream of cars and buses loaded with leaf peepers.

For savvy hikers, autumn is a great excuse to check out some of Maine's best hiking trails as well as the changing leaves.

Acadia/Down East

Home to Acadia National Park and the Bold Coast, eastern Maine has some of the most developed—and most easily accessible—trail networks in the state. For a foliage photographer, the region also offers supersaturated colors as the first rays of sun in the country hit Maine, making the leaves burn yellow, red, and purple.

On Mount Desert Island, the summit of Cadillac Mountain allows for dramatic views of Bar Harbor, Acadia, and the Cranberry Islands. Hikers can reach the peak via the 7.4-mile South Ridge Trail (which climbs from just south of the Blackwoods entrance on Route 3) or the easier, 4.4-mile open climb on the North Ridge. Drivers and bikers can ascend the 3.5-mile paved road to the Cadillac summit.

Acadia's 57-mile network of carriage roads won't lead travelers to mountaintop vistas, but certainly will provide close views of colorful spruce, birch, and maple trees. The copingstones, lodges, and stone bridges on the carriage roads are framed by the foliage, as are the many lakes that border the trails.

Farther east, the 5.5-mile loop of the Bold Coast Trail in Cutler in-cludes 1.5 miles that hug sheer, ocean-side cliffs. The colors aren't as bold as in other parts of the state, as the trees tend more toward evergreen than deciduous. Still, the incredible cliffs make up for the dimmer colors.

Western Mountains

By following Route 4, you can reach a handful of hikes that showcase this region.

Tumbledown Mountain in Weld—or more accurately, in Township 6—is one of my favorite hikes in the state any time of the year. During autumn, the hill is ablaze with color. The steep but satisfying Brook Trail takes hikers up a nearly vertical two miles to Tumbledown's unique alpine pond. From the pond, trekkers can fairly easily climb to the surrounding North, East, and West Peaks.

Up the road a piece, in Township E, just south of Rangeley, Smalls Falls gives the less athletically inclined among us a much easier hike. Less than half a mile up a boardwalk from the Smalls Falls rest area, visitors can see three-, twelve-, fourteen-, and twenty-five-foot waterfalls. The foliage isn't the only colorful attraction, as the stone in the gorge offers a rainbow of colors. Greg Parsons and Kate Watson, authors of *New England Water-falls,* spotted "beiges, oranges, greens, blacks, browns, gold, and ivory."

Portland and Southern Maine

As the colors begin to fade in the mountains and Down East, the foliage in southern Maine will reach its fiery peak. Covered in small mountains and foothills, the region is a haven for hikers with families, or those looking for quick, easy hikes.

In Sebago, Douglas Mountain offers big views with little effort. The Ledges Trail is the most direct route up, but its steepness is balanced by the fact that it's only a quarter-mile hike. The Woods and Eagle Scout Trails are slightly longer, but have a more gradual grade. From the stone tower atop Douglas, on a clear day you can see foliage clear from Sebago to Mount Washington.

Rattlesnake Mountain, off Route 85 in nearby Raymond, is about the same length and difficulty as Douglas. There's no tower at the summit, but two overlooks on the route up provide great views of the Sebago-area lakes.

For easy hikes that provide opportunities for bird-watchers as well as leaf peepers, the Audubon sanctuaries that dot southern Maine are easily accessible and meticulously maintained. Mast Landing in Freeport, Gilsland Farm in Falmouth, and Scarborough Marsh are minutes from Portland, and their trails cover many wooded miles.

No matter where you choose to travel in the fall, Maine holds some of the nation's most spectacular foliage. Take this opportunity to hike through it, if you can, rather than viewing it from afar.

ON THE WATER

II

Back on the Bay

IKNOW I'VE MADE THE TRANSITION from winter to spring when I
hang up the skis—except for one last trip scheduled to the East Snow-
fields on Mount Washington in early June—and slip the kayak off the
Jeep and nudge it into the still chilly waters of Penobscot Bay for my traditional inaugural April paddle.

The excitement starts to build around Easter Sunday, the day I annually pull the kayak off the wall in the barn and mount it in the rack on
the car roof in anticipation of my first spring excursion. This premature
preparation usually results in quizzical glances from folks in the parking lots
at Sugarloaf and Saddleback, my springtime skiing haunts, not to mention
the odd appearance of a snow-covered kayak from a late-season storm. I
just want to be sure I'm ready if an especially warm day in April suggests
that it's time to hit the water. Like I still feel on Christmas Eve, or when
the first snow arrives in November, I have a hard time sleeping the night
before my first planned kayak trip of the season.

Penobscot Bay, more often than not, is where I begin my paddling season, for a variety of reasons. First, it's close enough to my mid-coast home
to allow me to get out on the water early to allow for a long, leisurely day
loosening up and exercising some atrophied upper body muscles that feel
like they've been in a six-month hibernation.

Equally important, I like to save unexplored water for later in the
summer and begin my season in the arms of an old familiar friend. My
love affair with Penobscot Bay goes back more than seventy years, from
my childhood growing up in Camden to years spent in our lobster boat
exploring every gunk hole from Port Clyde to Stonington. My familiarity

with that spectacular stretch of the Maine coast provokes me to feel not just at home, but very comfortable.

I was going to launch from the working wharf on the snug little working harbor in Owls Head. There was a breeze out of the east kicking up two- to four-foot seas, and the temps were hovering around fifty degrees, but I was dressed and prepared and the bright sun made for a very comfortable paddle—especially for the first day out. A family of ducks accompanied me as I headed out of the harbor north toward Owls Head Lighthouse, past some summer cottages still boarded-up for winter, and the ever-present seagulls that had followed the lobster boats in decided to spend a little time socializing with me.

Out around Dodge Point and inside of Dodge Point Ledge, as the tide was nearing its peak, I made my way inside of the marker on Owls Head Ledge and the classic lighthouse loomed ahead. It took only a few hundred yards and an equal number of strokes before it felt like I'd never left the water, and I was reminded of the old adage about getting back on the bicycle. You might not remember what to do, but your body, thankfully, will. Some spray over the deck, and the roll of the kayak as the swells built out around the lighthouse reawakened the dormant sensations that conspire to make ocean kayaking the enjoyable and stimulating experience that it never fails, at least for me, to be.

Turning south at the light, I rode the rollers back down along the lee-ward side of Monroe Island—I felt that testing the ocean side of the island could wait for a subsequent visit. As I paddled by the variegated western shore, I was reminded of a trip long ago when I watched in fascination as a large doe swam effortlessly toward the island from the mainland.

Staying inside of Sheep Island, and making the mental note to return once again to the sheltered, sunset-facing beach on its westerly shore before the summer was over, I crossed over Sheep Island Bar and took a bearing to Hendrickson Point before scooting back up past Holiday Beach—empty and quiet on this chilly April day—and then back to my launch spot in the harbor.

Not an especially long and exhausting paddle, but the perfect start to a summer of pleasure on the water.

Androscoggin Adventure

WITHIN A SHORT DRIVE OF MORE THAN HALF the population of Maine, and the sound of the traffic on Route 1 the only reminder that civilization is near, this special kayaking adventure will come as more than a surprise. It's a reminder that even in the most unexpected places, another Maine resource is just waiting to be explored.

Although I had seen the occasional kayaker paddling the Androscoggin River just below the bridge for busy Route 201 between Topsham and Brunswick, and had filed away the thought that there could be some interesting paddling there—not to mention that there were always fishermen either on the banks or out on the water—I realized as I put in my kayak at the convenient and well-marked municipal launch site just below the bridge on the Brunswick side of the river, that I was in for a treat.

Whether you want to paddle for a few hours or a full day—if you have the time and energy—this stretch of water running for about five miles down to Merrymeeting Bay stands ready to reward you with some surprising variety, landscape, and exploration opportunities.

I suggest that you check a local tide chart so you can plan your trip downriver to coincide with the ebbing tide and your return upriver on the incoming flow. The combination of the river current and an outgoing tide can make the return trip a little strenuous, as I found out on my first day on the river.

If you're new to kayaking, it's worth remembering that a long paddling trip can be made a lot easier and less tiring if you constantly remind yourself to exert more pressure on your paddle by pushing with your upper hand than by pulling with your lower—it may seem counterintuitive for some canoe aficionados, but, believe me, it'll pay off.

As I pushed away from the launch site, I couldn't resist paddling upstream to the rapids just below the dam, to both enjoy the view and briefly ride the swirling water downstream as the perfect start to my trip down to the bay.

My first pleasant surprise as I headed down the river was the sight of several islands that seem to literally fill the river: Cow, Cornish, Driscoll, and some smaller ones that you could spend an entire day exploring. Except for the traffic sounds in the distance, and the warm water, you can almost imagine that you're somewhere in the North Maine Woods.

The kayak is the perfect craft for this stretch of the Androscoggin River, as sandbars abound and some of the passages between and around the islands are only a few inches deep. I'd encourage you to take the time to meander among the mixed-forest islands as I did.

But the bay was my destination, so I headed northeast past Mustard and Freyer Islands into the opening expanse of Merrymeeting Bay, where six rivers converge, forming a 9,000-acre wonderland of mudflats and sandbars upon which wild rice and pickerel weed flourish. Home to several species of endangered and protected wildlife, the bay offers sightings of bald eagles and ospreys, and fishermen will find shad, smelt, striped bass, river herring, and salmon.

Perhaps most famously, Merrymeeting Bay and its tributaries are favored breeding grounds for Canada geese, herons, and other wading birds, not to mention many species of ducks.

One departing suggestion: Plan your Androscoggin paddle for an early Sunday morning—if the tides cooperate—so you can end your trip with a visit to the Sea Dog Brewing Company in the old Bowdoin Mill in Topsham, where you can sample their sumptuous buffet brunch. It alone is worth the trip.

Paddling Merchant's Row

S EA KAYAKERS HAVE LOTS OF OPINIONS about their favorite paddles
on the coast of Maine, but my unscientific polling has revealed that
to a person they agree that the archipelago comprised of some forty
islands in the thoroughfare between Stonington and Isle au Haut provides
the most variety and opportunity for exploration, not to mention sheer
beauty, of any water on the coast. Add to that the unique charm of the
working village of Stonington, stuck out on the end of Deer Isle, and the
rugged coastline of Isle au Haut some seven miles off shore, and you've
got a combination of attractions that will capture you and command you
to return again and again.

Stonington isn't hard to find, but it is a way off the beaten path—good
news for those of us who like to have some of our summer more or less
to ourselves. Not to say that Deer Isle hasn't been discovered—the main
street often bustles with tourists during the peak summer season—but
many are there to take the mail boat to Isle au Haut for a day on the island
enjoying the hiking in the section of Acadia National Park that makes up
60 percent of the island.

Most people get to Deer Isle by following Route 15, which leaves
Route 1 in East Orland a few miles east of Bucksport. This route takes you
through the charming village of Blue Hill at the base of Blue Hill. It's close
to thirty miles from Route 1 to the end of the island, the last ten after you
cross the bridge to Little Deer Isle and a causeway joining it to Deer Isle.
You'll often see kayakers in the cove, and sunbathers on the beach there,
and it's a protected spot for paddlers not quite up to tackling the more
exposed waters farther out in the bay.

The public launch site in Stonington is the place to start your adventure. Then it's a question of which islands and which thoroughfares to strike out for. Every island beckons with white and pink granite sloping down to the water from densely wooded interiors, and tiny beaches dot the shores. Even the names add to the temptation to explore: Grog, Round, Sprout, Potato, Enchanted. Though in some cases the names might encourage you to paddle on: Hell's Half Acre, Devil, Wreck. You'll see old quarries on some of the islands and the remains of stone piers that once bustled when the granite trade was booming, and there is a rejuvenated quarrying operation on Crotch Island. A word of caution though, many of the islands are privately owned and visitors aren't welcome. But Wreck, Round, Mc-Glathery, and Russ belong to environmental groups, and many others are part of the Maine Island Trail where paddlers are welcome. Just pick up a chart at a local store, or go the Maine Island Trail's website.

The tight passages between the islands, which lobstermen approach with trepidation in their lobster boats, make for ideal kayaking, and the plethora of coves and harbors calls you to stop for a while just to soak up the scenery.

Once you reach Isle au Haut, you're in the footsteps of Samuel de Champlain, who discovered, explored, and named the island nearly four hundred years ago. And there's evidence that Native Americans inhabited the island more than 6,000 years ago. Because of the abundant fish in the waters around the island, the population grew to 275 souls by the late nineteenth century, but by 1935, the number had diminished to just seventy-five people. And the 2000 Census revealed that the year-round population had grown by only four to seventy-nine residents. But thanks to rusticators and others from away who were drawn to the island's rugged beauty, the 1880s saw vacation cottages being built in the village on the thoroughfare between the island and neighboring Kimball Island. So the population now doubles in the summer, but stays well within manageable limits.

For folks who don't want to paddle, the Stonington mail boat's regular schedule gets them out to Isle au Haut and back, stopping not only in the village but around on the west side in tiny Duck Harbor, where you can pick up a hiking trail to explore the park and make your way to the bold east end with its commanding view.

The island is six miles long and two miles wide, and its most prominent features—with wonderful hiking opportunities—are Mount Chamberlain, Rocky Mountain, and Sawyer Mountain, each of which are in the five-hundred-foot range. These mountains are clearly visible from the Camden Hills as they rise on the eastern horizon and are no more than thirty miles away as the crow (or the osprey) flies across East Penobscot Bay.

There's even a small freshwater lake, Long Pond, on the west side of the island.

One could argue that to kayak the islands of Merchant's Row is to taste the quintessential Maine coast experience, and that wouldn't get an argument from me.

Info, maps, and so forth:

www.isleauhaut.com
www.deerisle.com
www.mita.org

Paddling the Chain of Ponds

S OME FORTY-FIVE MILES UP SCENIC ROUTE 27 from Kingfield lies a magical unit of the Maine Public Reserved Lands comprised of five interconnected ponds ideal for kayaking and fishing.

On one trip, I found some idyllic paddling and, although the recent warm weather had sent the fish a little lower than my dry flies could attract, I did find a stretch in some rapids just below the dam on the lowest of the ponds where I managed a few strikes.

Getting to the Chain of Ponds is almost half the fun, as you drive from Kingfield to Sugarloaf along the bank of the Carrabassett River and over two new bridges replacing those taken out by the torrential rains of Hurricane Irene a couple years ago.

From there, it's another thirty miles through Stratton, past the end of Flagstaff Lake in Eustis, and up the Arnold Trail along the Dead River nearly to the Canadian border in Coburn Gore. Along the way, there's a pretty little rest stop at Sarampus Falls before you hit a winding road along the east side of the ponds.

It's worth remembering that this is the preferred route for trucks hauling logs, lumber, wood chips, and other cargo to and from Canada. The drivers don't seem interested in enjoying the scenery, so caution is advised as they barrel along toward their destinations.

It's about three hours from Portland or Bangor to the ponds, and it makes for a pretty long day trip. You might consider camping at the wonderfully situated and appointed Natanis Point Campground, located on a spit of land bordering the two upper ponds, Round and Natanis. Comprised of sixty-one grassy sites capable of accommodating tents to big RVs, Natanis Point has both shorefront and wooded sites strategically placed and separated to provide a perfect north woods camping experience. There's even a remote site reachable only with a paddle on Round Pond that provides just the kind of seclusion that some campers really appreciate.

There is also a 900-foot sandy beach on Natanis Pond, hiking on nearby Snow and Kibby Mountains and, for ATVers, direct access to about 150 miles of backcountry riding.

But it's the kayaking that draws me to the chain, as the five-mile run from north to south starting at Round Pond under the bridge leading to the campground, then down Natanis, Long, Bog, and Lower Ponds is a paddler's delight. Islands dot the ponds and provide scenic variety while steep bluffs and cliffs along the way add to the allure.

Since all of the ponds are interconnected, no portaging is required, and, although on my last trip there were some whitecaps on Natanis stirred up by a stiff southeasterly breeze, the ponds are well-protected and generally very serene.

I was in my smaller freshwater kayak (better as a fly-fishing platform but sans spray skirt) for that trip, and I got pretty wet heading into the breeze on Natanis. So I opted to put my kayak back on the Jeep and drive down to the dam on Lower Pond and head back up the chain from south to north. That turned out to be a great choice as the lower ponds were pretty placid, and I was able to see a few remote campsites within the Reserved Lands jurisdiction that beckoned for a future overnight trip.

If you choose to launch at the dam on Lower Pond, look carefully for an unmarked gravel road on the left just a couple of hundred feet north of the Gold Brook Road and the bridge over the brook. The road is marked with a large sign indicating it's the route to the Kibby Mountain Wind Power Project—some of the turbines can be seen as you paddle.

After finishing my day on the water, I uncased my rod and cast for a while in the rushing waters below the dam. For me, a fish striking my fly is nothing more than a bonus, the real pleasure was in savoring the rhythm of the sport and enjoying the sounds of the stream as it dropped over the dam to the accompaniment of songbirds in the trees. It provided the perfect coda to a day in the kayak.

Delightful Donnell Pond

I ALWAYS SAVE A FEW OF MY FAVORITE freshwater paddles for September and October to drink in the autumn colors and to imprint some lasting images in my mind to savor by the fire over the winter months as I anticipate the next summer.

High on my list is Donnell Pond, located in Maine's Public Reserve about twelve miles east of Ellsworth via Route 1, and then either Route 182 or 183, depending on where you want to access the pond. It's easy to find and rewards you with some of the best paddling you'll find.

The easiest place to put your kayak or canoe in the water is at a launch site about a mile east on Route 182, a short distance after passing through the village of Franklin. Just keep your eye out for a right turn directly after passing a pizza shop. That'll put you on the Donnell Pond Road, which leads directly to a launching area with a large parking lot, an information kiosk, and even a privy.

Another option for launching is off Route 183 on a road that brings you to the south end of the pond, the start of the Schoodic, Black, and Caribou Mountain hiking trails, and Schoodic Beach. The downside of this second route is that you'll have to lug your boat about half a mile to get to the water.

A paddle to the east out of the beautiful cove at the Route 182 launch site brings you to a point where the pond heads south to Schoodic Beach and the trail up Schoodic Mountain, should you decide you'd like to do some hiking. Before you get to the beach, you'll pass a couple of remote campsites along the west shore beckoning you to consider camping there on your next visit.

Pushing off from Schoodic Beach, and paddling north on the east side of Donnell Pond, you'll reach Redman's Beach, where there are some day-use picnic areas and three beautiful campsites. This part of the preserve is also reachable via a trail over Black Mountain from Schoodic Beach, and some campers will hike the nearly three miles to enjoy the remoteness, seclusion, and beauty of these picturesque sites.

But for the paddler, the beach represents either a great stopping-off point to enjoy a rest, lunch, and a swim before continuing around the pond, or a place to set up camp for the night. The three sites have picnic tables, fireplaces, and a centrally located privy, so you're provided with all the conveniences for an overnight or longer stay. By the way, you are limited to fourteen consecutive days in any forty-five-day period. Although I've never camped there, each time I go I'm reminded to add it to my list for the next summer.

The campsites here are remote enough that one of them will almost certainly be available should you hike or paddle there, and an added bonus is that as you settle down for the night in the shadow of Black Mountain, you get to enjoy the sunset over Schoodic Mountain to the west over the pond.

The entire shoreline is worth exploring, as large boulders in the shallow water and several small islands offer some scenic splendors that make this pond a very special paddle. So, after heading north from Redman's Beach, hug the east shore as you head all the way around Martins Ridge Cove before heading back to your launch site.

On my last visit, the only other boat on the entire pond was an early morning fisherman out to try his luck, and you'll never be disturbed by a Jet Ski, as they aren't permitted on this special body of water. All in all, Donnell Pond is a perfect way to wind down another summer of great paddling.

Paddling the Magalloway and Androscoggin Rivers

I F YOU ONLY PLAN ON ONE RIVER PADDLE during the summer, let me suggest that you consider a delightful trip along the Maine–New Hampshire border, starting in Wilsons Mills, Maine, down the Magalloway River into Umbagog Lake, and then down a short section of the Androscoggin to Errol, New Hampshire. However, before you head either to the headwaters across Route 16 from Oquossoc or over to the take-out through Grafton Notch from Bethel, you're faced with a couple of decisions.

First, will it be a canoe or kayak excursion? There's a lot to recommend either option, and my family has done both for very good reasons. A canoe allows you to travel in the company of a companion and, for me, it provides a more stable platform for fly-fishing. Slightly more difficult to propel than a kayak, especially if you plan to do any upstream paddling, a day on the water in a canoe is still hard to beat.

A kayak, on the other hand, glides seemingly effortlessly through the water, especially with the current, and I'm always amazed at the difference in perspective as I sit at water level, and I always feel slightly more at one with the environment than if I'm sitting a foot above the surface in a canoe seat. But maybe that's just me.

The second important choice is whether to take along two vehicles, leaving one at the take-out to provide transport back to your launch site. If you only take one, there's a fair chance you can hitch a ride to your car on the well-traveled road, especially if you're seen on the shoulder carrying a paddle. But it's a chance I've yet to take.

A third decision you'll need to make is whether to start your trip in New Hampshire—which will require you to paddle against the current—or in Maine. Our first trips on the waterway were short forays up the Androscoggin for a few miles on calm, slow-flowing water from a launch site a couple of miles north of Errol. Whether you're paddling from here upstream or nearing the end of a downstream paddle, a stop at L.L. Cote on the way is a must. Errol's answer to L.L. Bean, Louise and Luc Cote's L.L. Cote offers an eclectic mix of fishing gear, clothing, food, firearms, boats, snowmobiles, hardware, and assorted goodies and sandwiches.

The paddle up to Umbagog Lake is about five miles, and you're assured of seeing not only various wildlife, but some eagles at the confluence of the Magalloway and Androscoggin just as you enter the lake. One year, in fact, we were treated to the sight of American and golden eagle pairs, and their young, circling and feeding on, we were advised by some other paddlers, the carcass of a dead moose on a sandbar.

Shortly after arriving at the lake, a turn north takes you into the Magalloway, and you can paddle upstream as long as your energy and time allow, before turning to drift back to your launch site.

Taking two vehicles, or opting for the chance to pick up a ride back to your car, allows you to experience the best of both rivers.

The best place to launch for the downriver trip is the grassy slope next to the bridge on Route 16 in Wilsons Mills. You'll reach this point heading west from Oquossoc past the dam on Lake Aziscohos. The water level— and your speed—will vary depending on whether or not there has been a release from the dam a few miles north of where you put in. You may even encounter a few skilled whitewater kayakers who've tested their technical skills in the rapids above. But your best family outing will start below the difficult section above the bridge.

This section of the Magalloway moves fairly rapidly, even when there hasn't been a dam release, and in only a few minutes, and after a couple of miles, you'll pass under a covered bridge near a charming camping area that has never, in our experience, appeared to be too crowded.

From there it's ten miles or so on the water to the bridge across the river at the Maine–New Hampshire border, then a few miles south to the offices of the Umbagog National Wildlife Refuge in Wentworth Location.

This is also a good spot to begin your first trip on the two rivers, as there's a parking lot and launch site here that will allow you to put in and paddle about eight miles to Umbagog Lake. This option also works best if you take two cars, and makes for a wonderful opportunity to experience

about thirteen miles of scenic slow-flowing beauty and lots of wildlife between Wentworth Location and the take-out above Errol.

The Umbagog Wildlife Refuge comprises more than ten miles of shoreline on the two rivers and much of 7,000-acre Umbagog Lake. Refuge
guidelines ask paddlers to refrain from disturbing or harming wildlife in
the area and, during the April–July nesting and breeding season, to stay in
the center of river channels and avoid hugging the shoreline or exploring
the backs of coves. You're also urged to stay out of nesting areas that are
indicated with signs.

The trip downriver to what is known as Leonard Pond, the complex
of islands and channels at the confluence of Umbagog Lake and the Magalloway and Androscoggin Rivers, is a paddler's paradise, featuring two
logans and an oxbow where you're apt to spot moose and great blue herons. Among the waterfowl you might encounter are ospreys, black and
ring-necked ducks, mergansers, and one of the highest concentrations of
nesting loons in New Hampshire.

Remember, if you plan to fish along the way, you'll need licenses for
both Maine and New Hampshire. Two states, two rivers, and an abundance of nature's wonders await the paddler who ventures west to this
special treasure.

More information, maps, and pictures: www.fws.gov/northeast/lakeum
bagog

Fun in Friendship

PADDLING A KAYAK IN FRIENDSHIP HARBOR on a quiet September morning it's hard to believe that this was the same place that was raided twice during the French and Indian War in the mid-1700s, and settlers were killed and scalped as they sought refuge on Garrison Island.

Or that this now picture-perfect coastal Maine community bustled in the late 1800s with a population not much less than its current 1,200 or so people, and featured two shipbuilders, two gristmills, a shingle mill, three sawmills, and assorted manufacturers of sails, carriages, boots, and shoes.

And it was those shipbuilders who incorporated the lines of Gloucester fishing vessels into the now world-renowned Friendship Sloop. The early sloops ranged in length from twenty to fifty feet, with the average sloops running between thirty and forty feet. They shared the same elliptical stern, and most had a clipper bow and were gaff rigged. The one thing they all shared was a preset formula: the beam equaled one third the overall length, and the length of the mast equaled the overall length plus half the draft. At the turn of the century, they were used in seining for herring, hand-lining for cod, swordfishing, mackereling, and, of course, lobstering.

So, one September morning, I paddled among some of these classics as well as modern-day lobster and cruising boats, as I drank in the beauty of the harbor, the village, and the islands. Although it was "thickafog," in the lobstermen's vernacular, the ghosts of Friendship's past appeared as I paddled past, not the least of them being *Gladiator*, a still-beautiful sloop built in 1902, lying on her mooring.

Kayaking Friendship and Muscongus Bay is a special treat, regardless of the weather, and it's easy to get there. From the south, it's only about a dozen miles down Route 220 from Waldoboro, and about the same distance down Route 97 from South Warren and Thomaston if you're coming from the north.

When you reach the center of the tiny village, take the Bradford Point Road at the Hahn Community Center for about a mile to a public launching site. At low tide, you can walk to Garrison Island. I like launching there instead of at the town landing on the harbor, as this gives you a wonderful view of the harbor as you either pass inside Garrison Island when the tide's in or out around it if it's out.

Friendship Long Island provides great protection so you'll often find placid paddling even when the seas outside are running a little high, and exploring its entire perimeter is a half day of some of the best coastal kayaking you'll find anywhere. Ospreys circle and cry, seals bask, and other seabirds fill the air. You'll see lobstermen at work, pulling traps or unloading their catch and taking on bait at the Co-op. Out around the south end of Friendship Long Island you'll pass inside Cranberry Island and head back along the east side to your launch site.

If the seas are favorable, and you're up for more serious ocean kayaking, you might consider paddling six miles out to the Franklin Island National Wildlife Refuge, part of the Maine Coastal Islands National Wildlife Refuge Complex. The twelve-acre island supports nesting gulls, eiders, black-crowned night herons, Leach's storm-petrels, and ospreys. But you can only go on the island during daylight hours between September 1 and March 31—it's off limits from April through August, the seabird nesting season. So plan an early spring or fall trip to this natural treasure.

After enjoying your cruise in the kayak, it'll be time to spend a while in the village soaking up the ambiance of a quintessential small coastal Maine community.

A stop at Archie Wallace's Groceries and Provisions in the middle of town is a must. The juxtaposition of an old-time country store and a modern deli with choice meats and cheeses makes for a very special place. Many places in Maine claim to serve "Maine's Best Lobster Roll," but at Archie Wallace's they don't make such a claim, they just do it!

Lying as it does on a peninsula jutting out into the Gulf of Maine between Muscongus Bay and the Friendship River, the fact that some 55 percent of the town's thirty-one square miles is water says a lot about it. It's connected to the sea in a very special way, and a day in a kayak exploring its hidden nooks and crannies should be on every kayaker's summer schedule.

On the Harraseeket River

I ONCE MADE THE SAME MISTAKE many paddlers make the first time they set out to explore the Harraseeket River and the beautiful stretch of Casco Bay surrounding South Freeport. I failed to consult the tide chart and arrived at the well-marked public launch site next to Falls Point Marine at dead low tide. There was literally no water in sight—only a trickle through some mudflats leading out to possible paddling several hundred yards away.

So, a word to the wise: plan your paddle within about three hours of high tide to assure an easy launch and a safe return. There's even a warning sign at the launch site, obviously presented for the naïvest of us, that we should only launch on a tide that will allow us to get easily back to shore as there's no water at low tide.

With that newly acquired wisdom, I set out a week later for one of the more delightful summer paddles on a stretch of water I'd only seen from my lobster boat many years ago, or from the deck of Harraseeket Lunch and Lobster as I enjoyed one of their famous lobster rolls.

After launching I headed down the shore on the right for a nice workout as I paddled against the incoming tide, past an osprey guarding her chicks on a nest atop a ledge marker just east of the Freeport town landing in South Freeport.

The busy harbor was full of pleasure craft, and I was reminded of a conversation I'd had with an old sailor friend on a chairlift the previous winter. When I remarked that I had a goal to ski as many days each year as my age, he said that his sailing buddies had a goal of always having a boat as many feet in length as their age. It looked as if there were a lot of older sailors mooring their sailboats in South Freeport, as there were plenty of lengthy and pretty spectacular boats bobbing in the harbor.

After admiring the pulchritude of the watercraft, I headed southwest, noting the medieval castle-style tower that serves as a chief landmark for the harbor. I learned later that it was part of Casco Castle, a summer hotel built in 1903 by trolley car magnate Amos F. Gerald as an inducement for people to ride his trolley line from Portland. The hotel burned in 1914, leaving only the tower.

Next I took a bearing past Spar Cove to Staples Cove and a cruise around Winslow Memorial Park, as so many people have reported to me how much they enjoy camping at this exquisite campground.

Then it was over to the west shore of Wolfe's Neck and a nice long paddle, this time with the assistance of the still incoming tide, up the meandering Harraseeket to Mast Landing. Along the way, I stopped to watch a mother heron training her three snow-white chicks to fish in the river. This stretch of the river is navigable, even in a kayak, only within an hour or two of high tide, and some might find the cocoa-colored water resulting from the tides movement over the mudflats not too inviting, but it still makes for a delightful paddle.

My return trip to the launch site was pleasantly interrupted by a voice calling my name from a dock. It turned out to be an old Bowdoin buddy who was awaiting the arrival by boat of some of our good friends. The only downside to our chance, and very pleasant encounter, was that as I fumbled to capture the reunion on a camera which contained some wonderful pictures of the day I'd just enjoyed, it slipped out of my hand and sank to the bottom of the river, where it joined whatever other historical artifacts reside there.

The trip reminded me that special outdoor pleasures, both recreational and social, await us around virtually any corner here in Maine, and that all we need to do is take the time to get out and enjoy them.

Paddling the Pemaquid River

THE PEMAQUID PENINSULA AND VICINITY offer so many kayaking options it's tough to decide just where to put your boat in the water, and what direction to point it for a day of pleasant paddling. For me, weather is a principal determinant, as I've found that on some days the surf around the lighthouse on Pemaquid Point can be a little daunting, so I usually opt for calmer seas before heading out around the peninsula.

That said, there are lots of options, from the sheltered launch site right on the harbor at Colonial Pemaquid State Historic Site in Bristol to another in Round Pond for a paddle in Muscongus Bay. A tour of Fort William Henry offers an interesting trip back to Maine's earliest days, and is an educational diversion well worth the time while you're down that way.

From the sandy beach on Pemaquid Harbor, it's not a long shot across John's Bay to South Bristol on the next peninsula to the west, and you can spend a whole day exploring under the drawbridge there and out to Christmas Cove.

Recently, however, I spent a few hours on the placid and peaceful waters of the Pemaquid River, watching young families of Canada geese who had left their nests and mud turtles basking in the warm sun on logs and rocks in the river. It was my first trip on that particular stretch of water, and I was reminded, once again, that no matter how many places in Maine I've explored, there's always something new to discover.

For years I've passed by the well-marked launch site on Route 130 in Bristol Mills, remarking to myself every time that someday I ought to give that stretch of river a try. So, after I had spent a recent Friday out on the ocean cavorting in the waves with a buddy, the friendly and placid confines of the river were especially appealing to me.

The first thing that caught my eye as I loosened up by heading the short distance south to the dam that marks the southern extremity of available paddling water was the striking 200-year-old stone bridge spanning the river in Bristol Mills. Turning north, I paddled against the easy half-knot current, past numerous duck houses on poles in the river, and watched kingfishers dive for meals.

The occasional splash of a muskrat slipping into the water broke the silence, and the whirring of dragonflies added to the background music provided by happy songbirds in the trees along the shore. The narrow river, shaded by maples and spruce trees on the banks, widened as I headed north and narrowed again as I passed under a bridge on the Benner Road, about two and a half miles into my trip, before emerging into Biscay Pond.

On my next trip, when I have an entire day, I plan to put the kayak in at the Nobleboro boat launch near the head of Pemaquid Pond to drift downriver for ten miles on the "Pemaquid Paddle Trail" all the way to Bristol Mills. This will require two cars, but will be well worth the necessity.

The Nobleboro boat launch is 4.2 miles north of Damariscotta on Route 1. A short distance after passing Back Meadow Road and Tidewater Telephone Company on your right, take a right turn at the Nobleboro Boat Launch sign.

Not only does the Pemaquid River offer some great paddling, thanks to the Pemaquid Watershed Association, which has its origins in the Biscay Pond Association, formed thirty-seven years ago by residents concerned about unsound development on the Pemaquid Peninsula, there are also eight miles of hiking trails in the area maintained by the association and a nature center.

The Nature Center, a collaboration with the town of Bristol, is located in the pavilion at Pemaquid Beach Park. Open daily in July and August, the center offers exhibits and activities related to the natural history and ecology of the beach.

A visit to www.pemaquidwatershed.org, or to the association's office at 15 Courtyard Street, right above the Chamber of Commerce, in Damariscotta, will provide you with lots of info about both the organization and the recreational options within its jurisdiction.

Kayaking Cape Rosier

ALTHOUGH CAPE ROSIER LIES ONLY A FEW MILES, as the crow flies, from my boyhood home in Camden, and despite the fact I'd once taken a trip by boat to Castine while still in high school, I think the first time this unique Maine treasure entered my consciousness was at the first Common Ground Fair more than thirty years ago.

It was there that I was held in thrall by two heroes of the "back to the land" movement, the iconic Scott and Helen Nearing, who were telling the story of their move from Vermont in the early 1950s to Cape Rosier. Wanting to escape the ski development in that state, they bought a homestead where they eventually built a stone house, now open to the public. In 1954, they coauthored *Living The Good Life,* the best seller that became the bible for folks seeking a primer on how to live off, and appreciate, the natural world around us.

That encounter provoked me to take a trip to this still sparsely settled peninsula jutting into Penobscot Bay between Castine and Deer Isle. And it inspired me to make annual visits since then to this off-the-beaten-path beauty spot.

On the western shore of Cape Rosier, the Maine Bureau of Parks and Lands manages the Holbrook Island Sanctuary, comprised of a canoe and kayak launching site, a network of hiking trails through upland forests and along rocky shores, and an adjacent island. The real attraction is the 115-acre Holbrook Island itself, lying a little less than half a mile from the mainland portion, and a sheltered kayak paddle. On the mile-long island there are few vestiges of the long history of human occupation. Instead, there are now open fields, dense evergreen forests, rocky ledges, sandy beaches, and mudflats that invite you to spend the day.

History tells us that the island was first settled during the Revolutionary War by Captain Jesse Holbrook from Truro on Cape Cod. The tall pines on the island provided the masts for sailing ships being built in Castine. Anita Harris, the last member of the final family to occupy the island, passed away in 1985 and generously willed the island to the state of Maine, with the condition that it be maintained "as a wildlife and natural area . . . devoted wholly to the preservation of nature."

In keeping with her wishes, the island has been allowed to return to its natural state, and most of the buildings have been removed. In strict compliance with her bequest, the state forbids picnic facilities, motorized vehicles, commercial ventures, road construction, fishing, hunting, or trapping. The Nearings would be pleased!

You can also reach the island with a somewhat longer, but equally pleasant paddle, from the public landing in Castine, and out around Nautilus Island. Even if you choose the shorter kayak trip from Cape Rosier to Holbrook Island, you should plan a visit to Castine while you're in the area. It'll be an immersion in Maine history—occupied since the early 1600s, Castine is one of the oldest communities in North America and has been the site of numerous trading posts, forts, missions, and permanent settlements of France. It is also the site of what is still considered by some historians to be the worst naval defeat in U.S. history. When the British fleet came down from Halifax, Nova Scotia, in 1779, the American fleet was forced to retreat up the Penobscot River, where every vessel was scuttled. The crews, which included Captain Paul Revere, made their way back to Massachusetts on foot. Revere himself was court-martialed, but later exonerated.

You get to Cape Rosier by heading south from Bucksport on Route 175 to its intersection in North Brooksville with Route 176. There you'll turn right and follow the well-marked directional signs to the cape and the sanctuary. Bearing left when you arrive on the cape, you can head around the seaward side, past the Nearing homestead, through the village of Harborside, ending up at the spot to launch your kayak for the paddle to the island.

If you decide to start your adventure in Castine, you'll leave Route 175 south of Bucksport in West Penobscot at its intersection with Route 166, which will take you right into Castine.

Either way, you're in for a treat. If you're like me, you'll start making plans for another trip to do some more exploring of the surrounding shoreline. I suggest heading up the Bagaduce River from Castine to Bagaduce Falls, a round-trip of about ten miles, and a delightful paddle.

Information:

www.maine.gov/dacf/parks
www.castine.me.us

Muscongus Sound

IF YOU'RE LOOKING FOR A COASTAL PADDLE that will combine just about everything you'd want out of a day on the water, Muscongus Sound in the mid-coast must be on your list. A few hours spent exploring the shoreline and harbors will include anything you might ask for: spectacular scenery, seabirds, harbor seals, working lobster boats, sleek sailboats, attractive cottages with lawns and gardens running down to the water's edge, and even a little history. That is not to mention the chance to paddle around an island that is home to an internationally recognized Audubon Camp that has been dedicated to the study of birds and the coastal environment for three quarters of a century.

Your adventure starts as you turn south on Route 32 in Waldoboro and head down the Pemaquid Peninsula. After about fourteen miles, just past Bremen, you'll crest a hill and descend into the tiny village of Round Pond. The public boat ramp where you'll launch is well-marked and easily accessible right next to the local fishermen's co-op, where you'll see lobstermen unloading their catch. There's a little takeout stand where you can grab lunch and sit on the deck overlooking the harbor when you return from your paddle.

You'll probably be tempted to paddle the entire perimeter of the protected harbor just to admire the well-kept grounds of the cottages that dot the shoreline before you head out into the sound. Then, I suggest you head up the shore toward tiny Muscongus Harbor less than two miles to the north. After exploring the harbor, paddle up into Greenland Cove for another couple of miles past Ram Island before swinging around Hockomock Point, then circumnavigating Hog Island and the Todd Wildlife

Sanctuary, home of the Audubon Nature Study Camp, launched in 1936 to educate teachers and adult students. The storied faculty has included such notable wildlife educators and conservation leaders as Roger Tory Peterson and Rachel Carson, as well as Dr. Stephen W. Kress, an ornithology instructor who founded Project Puffin, the internationally acclaimed seabird conservation program. The camp is a leader in environmental education and attracts students from across the country to experience both the profound beauty and ecological significance of this unique Maine treasure. More than 20,000 K–12 teachers have studied in this natural classroom and experienced the magic of Hog Island.

If you have enough time, and the weather's right, consider exploring a couple miles farther north up the shore to Medomak, where, incidentally, there's a hand-carry launch site. You might be tempted to do some paddling around Bremen Long Island that protects Medomak a short distance to the east.

Heading south from Hog Island you'll arrive after about half a mile at Louds Island, with its stunning little Marsh Harbor in the shadow of Marsh Island. Then it's out around Bar Island off the south end of Louds. There's a sandbar off Louds that's barely covered with water at high tide. Local legend has it that this is the place where Wampanoag chief Samoset was buried. Historians tell us that Samoset was the first Native American to make contact with the Pilgrims on March 16, 1621, in Plymouth. He surprised them by strolling straight through the middle of their encampment and speaking English, learned from the foreigners he'd befriended who fished off Monhegan Island.

If you're especially energetic, you could continue south from Louds Island for another five miles past Long Cove Point, with a stop at the Rachel Carson Salt Pond Preserve before entering New Harbor, a rewarding destination that's an archetypical working harbor, full of lobster boats and draggers—not to mention a great waterfront seafood restaurant. Continuing even farther for another three miles to Pemaquid Point will probably be more than can be included in your one-day itinerary, but you'll want to plan a future visit. It's important to leave yourself enough time—and energy—to make the return paddle to your car.

Penobscot Bay Pearls

S TRUNG LIKE PEARLS ON A NECKLACE for about eight miles north to south from Islesboro's Gilkey Harbor in West Penobscot Bay lie eight delightful islands that beg to be explored by ocean kayakers.

As they're only about five miles off the coast between Camden and Lincolnville Beach, they can be easily reached from either a convenient launch site at the end of Sea Street on the east side of Camden Harbor—where's there's plenty of parking for your vehicle—or from the ramp at Lincolnville Beach.

My only caution, based on years of plying the waters of that particular piece of Penobscot Bay in my lobster boat, is that it often breezes up from the southwest in the afternoon, which can make your return trip a little choppy. So plan accordingly, and be sure you're equipped with a spray skirt to avoid a soaking.

Many people will take the state ferry, which makes several trips daily, from Lincolnville Beach to Islesboro and launch from there to explore south along the shores of the islands all the way to Mark Island at the end of the necklace.

You might consider planning a trip of a couple of days, and camp at Warren Island State Park, only a short paddle from the Islesboro launch site on Grindel Point. There are ten campsites, two Adirondack shelters, and plenty of fresh drinking water. And don't be concerned that all the sites will be taken when you arrive. Paddlers are never turned away. There is ample space in the park to accommodate all visitors, and the friendly staff will make sure you have a spot for the night. It's a beautiful little spruce-covered island, around which you'll certainly want to paddle, along with neighboring Spruce Island.

You might want to plan your excursion to coincide with an outgoing tide as you paddle down the chain and an incoming on the way back, but I've never found the tide to be much of an issue. Begin your exploration of the chain along the east shore of Seven Hundred Acre Island by heading south down Gilkey Harbor with views of the striking Dark Harbor estates on Islesboro to your east. After a quiet paddle in and around Cradle Cove, it's off to Minot Island and then south to Middle Island, which is connected to larger Job Island. In the middle of Job is a hill rising about a hundred feet above sea level. If you opt to go down the east side of Job, you'll pass through Bracketts Channel and by Pendleton Point on the southern extremity of Islesboro.

Then it's through the shallow water covering Lime Island Bar to beautiful Lime Island, a favorite picnic and swimming spot in my youth with my Camden chums as the property on the north end was owned by the parents of a classmate of mine.

I'd suggest paddling down the west side of Lime to neighboring Lasell, the one island in the lower section of the chain that has some habitation. In fact, if you find the beckoning beach on the north end of the island appealing, you might be interested to know that you can pick up an entire 36.6-acre chunk of land with about a mile of shorefront on that end for a mere $1,495,000!

Strung below Lasell are Saddle and then Mark Islands, which are small enough, and beautiful enough, that you'll want to circle each of them before heading back north. Bold rock outcroppings and ledges, tiny beaches for sea glass picking and seal spotting, and towering spruce trees distinguish both of these islands that best embody the coast of Maine. Chains of islands like those in West Penobscot Bay offer some of the best kayaking anywhere.

Prime Time for Rollin' on the River

WHITEWATER RAFTING IS JUST ABOUT THE MOST EXCITING way to experience the Maine wilderness. Hurtling down a river in a raft with half a dozen others is the all-natural version of a roller coaster. With a number of rafting outfitters and three of the most reliable rafting rivers in the East, Maine is a rafter's paradise. With cooler temperatures and scheduled high-water releases, there's no better time than the fall to try the sport.

Boating and rafting on Maine rivers has been a form of transportation for ages—longer, in fact, than horseback riding or many other forms of travel. The Maine economy also relied on the flowing rivers, with log drives bringing wood down to the coast. It's only in the past few decades that whitewater rafting has become a popular leisure activity.

Prior to 1976, log drivers were moving about 300,000 cords of wood a year down the Kennebec River. Changes to state law made it illegal to float logs down the Kennebec, helping to open up Maine rivers for rafters. Later that year, the first commercial rafting trip traveled the upper Kennebec. In the 1970s and 1980s, state legislation regulating safety and licensing established standards for commercial rafting companies on Maine rivers.

An allocation system was also put into place, regulating the number of people who could be on the rivers on any given day. This system wasn't a cap on supply to increase demand, but a move to protect the rivers of Maine from overuse. The rules governing whitewater rafting in Maine have helped the sport grow over the years. The Maine Warden Service reported just under 21,000 passengers in 1983. By 2009, that number had ballooned to 61,337.

Commercial rafting in Maine is focused on three rivers—the upper Kennebec River, the West Branch of the Penobscot River, and the lower Dead River. One feature shared by all three is hydroelectric dams above the spots where rafting companies "put in" for their trips. The dams, which conduct daily water releases, ensure that the rivers have enough water for rafting, even during lean, dry summers.

The Dead River has a number of "high-volume" releases every year. These big releases mean consistent action for the sixteen-mile stretch of the Dead that rafting outfits run. The Kennebec River usually has two September releases, sending out water at 8,000 cubic feet per second. These Kennebec River "flush trips" offer the biggest rapids possible in Maine.

Though rafting trips vary from company to company, there is an outline that most outfitters follow. After an early morning start at the rafting company's base camps (most are based in the Forks), visitors will get a safety orientation and equipment, including helmets and life preservers. Since the base camps are typically downriver from the whitewater routes, shuttles take rafters and their equipment up the river to put in. The trips down the twelve-plus-mile runs are full-day affairs, and usually include a stop for lunch along the way.

You might suspect that whitewater is a young person's game, with only teens and twenty-somethings up for fighting punishing rapids. Not so, according to Raft Maine (raftmaine.com), an association of Maine's professional whitewater rafting outfitters. It points out that "people of all ages from eight to eighty with no previous experience" can go whitewater rafting. That said, most outfitters enforce a minimum suggested age—usually twelve to fifteen years old—on some of the burlier rapids.

Whitewater guides classify rapids in six categories, ranging from Class I (gently flowing water with few rapids and no obstacles) to Class VI (nearly impossible, life-threatening rapids only attempted by professionals). In Maine, thrill-seekers can find rapids up to Class V. For those less inclined to raging rapids, there are a number of easier trips that put in partway down the rivers.

Rafting combines the excitement of a roller coaster, an invigorating workout, and the breathtaking beauty of Maine's woods and rivers. While I'd suggest fitness and bravery before signing up, Raft Maine is correct that rafting is within the reach of people of all ages and experience levels.

Rediscovering Deboullie

I FEEL ESPECIALLY BLESSED that as a youngster growing up in Maine I was able to experience the best of both worlds: living and going to school on the coast in Camden in the winter and cutting my skiing teeth at the Camden Snow Bowl, and spending the first thirteen summers of my life in the North Maine Woods at a set of camps my grandfather, Dr. Arthur Christie had built on the west shore of Portage Lake, and at another compound on idyllic Island Pond in what is now the nearly 22,000 acres of the Deboullie Preserve in Maine's Public Reserve Lands system.

My first trip to Red River (officially named T15 R9) and the Deboullie country was with Herschel Currie, my grandfather's guide and camp care-taker, poling up through the rapids for more than ten miles from Portage Lake, then on horse and buckboard for another ten miles or more to the camps. It's an experience that has lived with me for nearly seventy years.

My last visit to Red River, prior to a couple of summers ago, was in 1954 when we flew in aboard a Super Cub from Portage. Today, you can access the area via a well-graded twenty-mile gravel road south from St. Francis, passing through (and paying a modest fee at) a North Maine Woods checkpoint. Or alternatively, you can head north out of Portage on a similar thirty-mile road. So it was with great excitement, more than fifty years since I had last been there, that my wife Marty and I packed up our camping gear and headed north for a trip down memory lane for me, and for her first look at a very important place in my life.

The good news: little has changed. Although the main lodge burned down a few years ago, the current owners have rebuilt it with a perfect log replica. Rather than stay at the camps, Marty and I chose to camp on the shore of Pushineer Pond, one of twenty-five lakes and ponds that are all within a five-mile radius of the camps. Most of the ponds are fly-fishing only, and four of them support a population of arctic char (black-backed trout) that came down in the Ice Age. Only ten bodies of water in the entire state are habitat to char.

A favorite pond of mine, Galilee, is not only great fishing, but sheer cliffs on one side provide a unique spectacle from the campsite. I still remember a mid-July day when I was very young and we were caught in a hailstorm there. Herschel leaned the aluminum canoe against a tree and we hunkered under it. What a sound!

Not to be missed on your visit to the preserve is a climb up Deboullie Mountain, a two-thousand footer, that, from the still-standing fire tower on the summit, provides a breathtaking view of the wild surroundings. From the end of Pushineer Pond, where the road ends, it's about a five-mile round-trip hike, but it can be shortened substantially by paddling to a campsite on the shore of Deboullie Lake.

Tom Hanrahan in his highly readable book, *Your Maine Lands: Reflections of a Maine Guide,* describes the climb this way:

> I begin my ascent with some trepidation. The climb is, in places, just short of technical climbing. In other words, a rope and some carabiners would probably come in handy. But I stumble into a cluster of purple trillium, and I marvel at the wildflowers. . . . I find some old telephone wire leading up to the fire tower and the old ranger's cabin. I keep climbing. I have more than 1,800 feet to go, most of it straight uphill. I pause often. But finally the summit is in sight, and when I crest the mountain I am rewarded with a vista that is a perfect summation of the Maine forest. Water is all around me.

Couldn't have said it better myself, Tom, old friend.

Info, maps, pics:

maine.gov/dacf/parks
redrivercamps.com
northmainewoods.org

Sandy River Ponds

A S MUCH AS I LOVE OCEAN KAYAKING, with the ever-changing face of the waters along the coast of Maine, come fall I head to a pristine pond or two, usually up in the western mountains, to catch the first autumn colors as they paint the hillsides.

One such trip took me to three tiny, interconnected ponds for what turned out to be one of the most pleasant paddles of the summer, as well as a chance to wet a fly in search of the elusive brookies that populate so many of Maine's remote bodies of water.

As I usually do when combining a paddle on placid inland waters with a chance to cast for trout, I'll pop into my comfortable little Old Town Dirigo 120 as the perfect platform for a fun day on the water. That proved to be an especially good choice on a recent trip, as some brief portages over and around some accumulated brush and a beaver's dam construction project were required to get to all three of the ponds I'd chosen for my outing.

Known as the Sandy River Ponds, they are a short distance above Madrid and below Rangeley on Route 4 in Sandy River Plantation. The middle of the three ponds is accessible via a well-marked launch site and parking area only a few minutes north of Smalls Falls and just beyond the Appalachian Trail crossing. It's a carry-in launch site only and requires a trek of about a hundred feet to the shore, but the little bit of effort required is well worth it.

The middle pond, about seventy acres in its entirety, is the largest, and deepest, at nearly sixty feet at the deepest point, providing some good cold water for trout habitat. It's open to fishing all summer, with no live bait allowed.

It's a short paddle from the launch site to the north end of the pond, then an easy maneuver, with a little dragging up the short connector between the middle and upper ponds. The latter totals only about twenty-eight acres, and its maximum depth of twenty feet is good habitat for chub, hornpout, and the usual warm water suspects such as perch and sunfish.

Heading south down the middle pond, you'll pass under a bridge on the Beech Hill Road and into another narrow and shallow passage to the lower pond, again requiring an easy portage. The lower pond is less than twenty acres, and a circumnavigation is possible in just a few minutes. A loon accompanied me around on my trip, adding to the unique charm of this little treasure.

The three ponds lie at an elevation of 1,700 feet, and are the headwaters for the 73.3-mile-long Sandy River as it cascades in its early stages on its rush down to Madrid, and then through Phillips, Strong, Farmington, and New Sharon on its winding journey to its confluence with the Kennebec River in Norridgewock.

There are lots of navigable stretches and launch sites along the river in Strong, Farmington, and Farmington Falls that attract paddlers from early spring through foliage season.

I also encourage you to stop at Smalls Falls after your paddle. The river is much wider above Smalls Falls, so there's a powerful rush of water through the narrower and interconnected set of four falls that make up one of Maine's most scenic rest stops.

A set of stairs takes you to a bridge at the base of the falls where there's a twenty-foot-wide circular pool into which the lower three-foot cascade drops. Above that, and viewable from the bridge, is a fourteen-foot horsetail at the base of which is a deeply carved oblong pool, which invites swimmers to jumping off the rocks above during the warm summer months.

Farther up there's another twenty-five-foot waterfall, above which is a twelve-foot horsetail featuring a smoothly worn slide. A trail, guarded by a chain-link fence, allows visitors to ascend the entire four-fall spectacle and drink in the beauty of nature at its most powerful and unrestrained.

It's a perfect way to spend an end-of-summer day in the Maine outdoors.

ON WHEELS, COMBINATION TRIPS, AND ALTERNATIVES

III

A Day on Dyer Neck

O N MANY TRIPS DOWN EAST WE NOTICED the signs for the Petit Manan National Wildlife Refuge on Petit Manan Point a few miles past Steuben on coastal Route 1 between Sullivan and Milbridge. Finally, on the way back from a few days camping on Campobello, we journeyed down Pigeon Hill Road on Dyer Neck to the refuge for a closer look. That short visit inspired me to return a few days later for a full day of hiking and kayaking in what is one of Maine's lesser-visited but captivating sanctuaries.

The Maine Coastal Islands National Wildlife Refuge spans more than 200 miles of Maine coastline and contains forty-nine offshore islands and four coastal parcels totaling more than 8,000 acres, of which Petit Manan Point is one. The National Wildlife Service manages these sanctuaries to provide habitat for colonial seabirds, such as common, Arctic, and endangered roseate terns, Atlantic puffins, razorbills, black guillemots, Leach's storm-petrels, laughing gulls, and common eiders. Wading birds and eagles also nest on the refuge islands, and on the mainland you can spot songbirds, seabirds, and waterfowl.

My day on Petit Manan Point included hikes on two scenic trails in the refuge and a climb up Pigeon Hill in a nearby 172-acre preserve managed and maintained by the Downeast Coastal Conservancy. The conservancy was formed a few years ago through a merger of the Great Auk Land Trust and the Quoddy Regional Land Trust, each with more than twenty years of experience protecting Maine's coastal lands for wildlife habitat and providing public access for recreational use. To date, the conservancy has protected more than 4,500 acres and forty-five miles of shoreline by working with conservation-minded landowners in the Down East region.

The 2,195-acre Petit Manan Point Division of the refuge features two separate hikes through stands of jack pine, coastal raised heath peat lands, blueberry barrens, old hayfields, freshwater and saltwater marshes, cedar swamps, granite shores, and cobble beaches.

The Hollingsworth Trail (6.2 miles down Pigeon Hill Road from Route 1) is a 1.5-mile loop with views of heaths and beaches. Interpretive signs along the way offer insights into refuge wildlife, habitats, and management. You're apt to hear and spot grassland birds such as bobolinks and savannah sparrows, and if you're there in the spring, you might spot an American woodcock in one of the clearings demonstrating his unique courtship display. Other resident wildlife make the refuge home year-round, and your chances of seeing a ruffed or spruce grouse, a white-tailed deer, snowshoe hare, porcupine, coyote, or raccoon are pretty good.

The longer Birch Point Trail, about four miles round-trip and a half mile closer to Route 1 than the Hollingsworth Trail, starts off in a blueberry field and leads to salt marshes on Dyer Bay after passing through a mixed-wood forest. Both hikes are pleasant strolls with great bird-watching opportunities and scenic vistas.

After my two hikes in the refuge and a short lunch, came the fun of exploring Pigeon Hill Bay and beautiful Bois Bubert Island in my kayak. I launched from a site where Pigeon Hill Road passes over a narrow spit of land dividing Pigeon Hill Bay from Carrying Place Cove.

If you have time, I'd suggest a circumnavigation of Bois Bubert Island in your kayak, where you'll be treated to perfect examples of Maine's rockbound coast at its best. In addition to interesting inlets and bays begging you to explore them, there's Little Bois Bubert Island off the south end that's great fun to paddle around. You'll also see the lighthouse on Petit Manan Island, which was maintained for more than a century by a resident light keeper, on the horizon off to the east, and there are commercial tour operators in the area who provide boat trips to view nesting seabirds on both Petit Manan and Machias Seal Island.

Heading back up the point toward Route 1, a sign on the left marks the trailheads for Pigeon Hill and its three short hikes: Summit Loop (0.3 miles), Silver Mine (0.4 miles), and Historic (0.4 miles). The reward from a short hike up Pigeon Hill is an amazing panoramic view stretching from Cadillac Mountain to the west and the Bold Coast to the east.

Off the beaten path, with the potential to immerse you in the best that the Maine coast has to offer, Petit Manan Point should be on your "must visit" list for fall or summer.

One Day, Two Mountains, and Two Lakes

I ALWAYS PLAN THIS DAY HIKE COMBINED with some wonderful paddling in the late spring before the traffic thickens on coastal Route 1. It involves not one, but two special mountains, easy enough to climb and close enough together that it's great fun to hike them both in the same day. And at the base of both hikes are two of Maine's prettiest ponds.

If you leave home early enough to be on the trail for the first climb by mid-morning, knocking them both off is a piece of cake, with time enough left for a relaxing paddle.

I always start on the one closest to my mid-coast home by heading to Bucksport and then turning off just six miles east of there on a side road to the north in Orland, a mile and a half after the junction between U.S. Route 1 and ME Route 15. The road is identified by a sign directing you to the Craig Brook National Fish Hatchery, about a mile and a half in on a paved, then gravel, road. There's parking at the hatchery, where you can leave your car to climb about six hundred vertical feet to the summit of Great Pond Mountain, sometimes referred to as Great Hill.

It's enough off the beaten path that you'll seldom encounter another hiker, despite the fact that the round-trip hike of a little over four miles rewards you with a quiet walk in the woods capped with exceptional views from the open summit.

When you get back to your car, a visit to the hatchery—America's oldest Atlantic salmon hatchery, established in 1871, is well worth the time. There you can see both hatchery raceways and a display pool, and study interesting displays and information on the propagation and research being carried out there.

Adjacent to the hatchery a boat launch ramp for Alamoosook Lake will catch your eye. I expect that if you feel there's not time enough for a paddle on this trip, you'll file it away for a future, longer visit.

But this is a two-hike day, so head east again on Route 1, and, in less than an hour after passing through Ellsworth and Franklin, you have a choice of two different routes up 1,069-foot Schoodic Mountain. The first is about four miles north of Sullivan on Route 200, leaving the road on the eastern side at the foot of a steep hill between two bridges in East Franklin. From there the hike to the summit is about two-and-a-half miles on a blue-blazed trail that takes you over open ledges as you approach the vestiges of the abandoned fire tower.

The second option, which I always take when Schoodic is the second hike of the day, is to continue driving a short distance on Route 1 to East Sullivan, then turn left on Route 183 and proceed four and half miles to a gravel road on the left, just after crossing some abandoned railroad tracks, where you'll spot a blue and white Public Lands sign. After about a third of a mile, take a left at a Y and it's a short distance to the Schoodic Beach parking lot. I always take the loop that goes first on a trail for about half a mile to the beach and campsites on the shore of pristine Donnell Pond, then a little more than another half mile from there to the summit on a trail that leaves from the western end of the beach. You can lug your canoe or kayak and put in at the beach, although it's easier to access the pond via the boat launch off Route 200.

The views of Frenchmans Bay and the surrounding countryside from the rocky and exposed summit are among the best you'll find. You'll see neighboring Tunk and Black Mountains, both of which are more than a thousand feet, and you'll want to file them away for future hikes. Both feature cliffs and steep ledges, and the trail up Tunk has been substantially improved in recent years.

Great Pond and Schoodic are two mountains that confirm you don't need to bag a 4,000-footer to be rewarded with some spectacular views.

Petit Manan Wildlife Refuge

ALTHOUGH ON MANY TRIPS DOWN EAST I had noticed the signs for the Petit Manan National Wildlife Refuge, on coastal Route 1 a few miles past Steuben between Sullivan and Milbridge, it was only recently, on the way back from a few days camping on Campobello, that I journeyed down Pigeon Hill Road on Dyer Neck for a closer look at the refuge.

That short visit inspired me to return a few days later to hike and kayak for a full day in what is one of Maine's lesser-visited but captivating sanctuaries.

The Maine Coastal Islands National Wildlife Refuge spans more than 200 miles of Maine coastline and contains forty-nine offshore islands and four coastal parcels totaling more than 8,000 acres, of which Petit Manan Point is one.

The National Wildlife Service manages these sanctuaries to provide habitat for colonial seabirds such as common, Arctic, and endangered roseate terns, Atlantic puffins, razorbills, black guillemots, Leach's storm-petrels, laughing gulls, and common eiders.

In addition to the many seabirds, wading birds and eagles nest on the refuge islands and on the mainland you can spot songbirds, seabirds, and waterfowl.

My day on Petit Manan Point included hikes on two scenic trails in the refuge and a climb up Pigeon Hill in a nearby 172-acre preserve managed and maintained by the Downeast Coastal Conservancy. The conservancy was formed through a merger of the Great Auk Land Trust and the Quoddy Regional Land Trust, bringing together two trusts, with more than forty years combined protecting Maine's coastal lands for wildlife habitat and providing public access for recreational use.

To date, the conservancy has protected more than 4,500 acres and forty-five miles of shoreline by working with conservation-minded land-owners in the Down East region.

Added to my hiking was the fun of exploring Pigeon Hill Bay and beautiful Bois Bubert Island in the kayak from a launch site where the road passes over a narrow spit of land dividing Pigeon Hill Bay from Carrying Place Cove.

The 2,195-acre Petit Manan Point Division of the refuge features two separate hikes through jack pine stands, coastal raised heath peat lands, blueberry barrens, old hayfields, freshwater and saltwater marshes, cedar swamps, granite shores, and cobble beaches.

The Hollingsworth Trail (6.2 miles down Pigeon Hill Road from Route 1) is a 1.5-mile loop with views of heaths and beaches. Interpretive signs along the way offer insights into refuge wildlife, habitats, and management.

You're apt to hear and spot grassland birds such as bobolinks and savannah sparrows, and if you go on a spring evening you might spot an American woodcock in one of the clearings demonstrating his unique courtship display.

Other resident wildlife call the refuge home, and your chances of seeing a ruffed or spruce grouse, a white-tail deer, snowshoe hare, porcupine, coyote, or raccoon are pretty good.

The longer Birch Point Trail, about four miles round-trip, and a half mile closer to Route 1 than the Hollingsworth Trail, starts off in a blueberry field and leads to salt marshes on Dyer Bay after passing through a mixed-wood forest.

Both hikes are pleasant strolls with great bird-watching opportunities and scenic vistas.

Heading back up the point toward Route 1, a sign on the left marks the trailheads for Pigeon Hill and its three short hikes: Summit Loop (0.3 miles), Silver Mine (0.4 miles), and Historic (0.4 miles).

The reward for a hike up Pigeon Hill is an amazing panoramic view from Cadillac Mountain to the west and the Bold Coast to the east.

If you have time, as I did on my full day, I'd suggest a circumnavigation of Bois Bubert Island in your kayak, where you'll be treated to Maine's rockbound coast at its best. In addition to interesting inlets and bays that beg you to explore, there's Little Bois Bubert Island off the south end that's fun to paddle around.

You'll see the lighthouse on Petit Manan Island on the horizon off to the east, and there are commercial tour operators in the area that provide boat trips to both Petit Manan and Machias Seal Islands, allowing visitors to view nesting seabirds.

Off the beaten path, and with the potential to immerse you in the best the Maine coast has to offer, add Petit Manan Point to your "must visit" list.

Kayaking (and Biking and Hiking)
Cape Jellison

C APE JELLISON, A 1,600-ACRE PENINSULA, juts out into Penobscot Bay just about where the bay begins to narrow into the Penobscot River flowing down from the Katahdin region through Bangor and along both sides of Verona Island. Back in Colonial days it was known as Wasaumkeag Point, and the remains of Fort Pownall, built in 1759 to protect the river, still stand sentinel there, along with Fort Point Lighthouse, built in 1836 and automated in 1988. The cape was also the site of the first port facility built by the Bangor and Aroostook Railroad.

Enough off the beaten path, and often overlooked by tourists and natives alike, I'm happy to share a little secret with you. If you're looking for a wonderful day's outing that might include kayaking, biking, hiking, fishing, sightseeing, and digging into Maine's colonial history, put a visit to the cape and Fort Point State Park on your list.

Keep your eye out for signs indicating the route to Fort Point State Park as you approach Stockton Springs, a few miles north of Searsport on coastal Route 1. After arriving on the cape, bearing right will take you shortly to an opportunity to launch your kayak on the east shore. From there, it's a delightful paddle out around the point to Fort Point State Park, which is on a small peninsula extending eastward from the cape, where you'll find a pier with floats and picnic tables with wonderful views up the river and across to the peninsula leading down to Castine.

One thing to bear in mind that those of us who've spent a lot of time on Penobscot Bay in the summer have come to expect is that it'll probably breeze up in the afternoon out of the southwest, which can make for a bit of a tussle getting back around the point to your launch site against the wind. And it'll be even more difficult if there's an incoming tide. So check the weather, the tide chart, and your watch so you don't get caught having a little more strenuous workout than you had planned.

On one breezy, sun-drenched morning, I was joined by a proud mother seal cavorting with her pup for a couple of miles as I ventured out through Stockton Harbor with Sears Island on my right. Paddling out around Squaw Point inside of Squaw Head, I was propelled by a nice westerly along the south side of the cape all the way to Fort Point with a nice view of the lighthouse.

Swinging around the point and heading back west, protected by the point from the increasing breeze, I put ashore on a sandbar for a snack. The tide was dead low, and from there I had a nice view of the rugged pier standing on the site of an old steamship wharf, where the Boston steamer used to pick up and drop off passengers. A couple hours wandering in the park energized me for the paddle back to my launch site.

The 120-acre Fort Point State Park features more than a mile of rocky shore, a tidal sandbar, and a diverse habitat for a variety of plants and animals. You can also to visit the Fort Point State Historic Site and the Fort Point Light Station. The remains of Fort Pownall contain interpretive panels and even a marker on the original burial site of General Samuel Waldo, for whom both Waldo County and the town of Waldoboro were named.

If your recreational pursuits for the day are land-based, the cape and the park have something to offer both hikers and bikers. There's a network of hiking trails that will take you through open fields and wooded areas to well-identified historic sites. Interpretive signs along the way describe the military and maritime history of the area, including the story of how 400 men under the leadership of Massachusetts governor Thomas Pownall labored to build the fort that, in his words, "would protect the finest bay on North America for large shipping just at the mouth of the Bay of Fundy and would be advancing the Frontiers of his Majesty's dominion."

Eventually though, his Majesty's forces seized the fort's cannons and powder in 1775. Later, a regiment of Continentals burned the blockhouse and filled in much of the ditch system to prevent the British from utilizing the fort, which they never were able to do.

If you brought along your bike, the seven-mile loop on the quiet road leading from the parking lot around the circumference of the cape makes for a relaxing ride on gentle terrain.

Information:

www.visitmaine.com/things-to-do/recreation-areas/fort-point-state-park/

A Day on the Quiet Side

MOUNT DESERT ISLAND IS ALWAYS A GREAT PLACE to spend some outdoor time, and my favorite part of that special island is "the quiet side" west of Somes Sound, where even in mid-summer, the trails on Acadia, Beech, Mansell, Bernard, and Western Mountains are uncrowded and the views are spectacular.

If you leave home early enough in the morning, or if you've spent the night near or on the island, you might want to combine, as I usually do, three wonderful diversions: sightseeing, hiking, and paddling.

I'd suggest bearing to the right on Route 102 at the intersection shortly after the causeway as you arrive on the island. This route will take you through picturesque Somesville and along the west shore of the sound for a short distance and then along the east shore of Echo Lake. You'll pass the road to Ike's Point on the lake, where there's a public launch site.

This is my chosen spot to launch the kayak for an early morning circumnavigation of the lake, with the most prominent visual feature being Beech Cliff along the southwest shore. It's always fun to paddle in its shadow knowing that, before the morning's over, you'll be scaling it to drink in the view down to the lake from high above. A couple hours exploring the shoreline of this small treasure of a lake make for a perfect morning.

Back in your car, proceed for a short distance to the road on your right leading to the parking lot and trailhead for the Beech Cliff Trail where your hike will start. You'll pass along the shore of Echo Lake briefly, then turn left to a steep, but short, ascent to the top of Beech Cliff. Take a right on the half-mile Beech Cliff Loop, where you'll be treated to a breathtaking view down to the lake and across to Acadia and St. Sauveur Mountains to the east. You'll want to include both of those mountains on a future trip.

Returning from the loop, turn right and proceed west for about a quarter mile to an intersection with the Valley Trail, which you'll follow south for another quarter mile to a well-marked intersection with the Canada Cliff Trail on your left. This mile-long trail proceeds first east and then turns north along the top of the cliffs for which it is named, sharing the same views as those from Beech Cliff.

You'll rejoin the Beech Cliff Trail, on which you'll turn right for the short scramble back down to your car. One of the rewards of this hike, if the weather's warm enough, is the sandy beach on Echo Lake just at the end of the trail. It's a great chance to cool off from your morning exertions.

Back in your car on Route 102, head south toward Southwest Harbor. After a little more than a mile, you'll pass Fernald Point Road on the left, which leads to Flying Mountain with its dominating view down to and across Somes Sound. If you have the time and the energy on this trip, I'd certainly recommend including a hike up the Flying Mountain Trail, then north on the Valley Cove Trail up the west shore of the sound. It's a little over two miles to the Valley Peak Trail, which will bring you back along the top of a set of cliffs to your starting point. If you can't include this circuit on trip, be sure to make plans for a future visit.

Then it's back on the road through Southwest Harbor. Assuming you've worked up an appetite, take the short trip down Clark Point Road to Beal's Lobster Pier, where you can dine on freshly caught and perfectly prepared seafood on a working dock overlooking the harbor.

Now for the sightseeing portion of your recreational trifecta. Leaving Southwest Harbor heading south, turn left on Route 102A through Manset, out around Seawall and on to Bass Harbor. Be sure to pop out to the oft-photographed Bass Harbor Head Light, where there's a short but rewarding hike on the Head Light Trail.

Proceed along quiet Route 102 through Bernard and Seal Cove back to the north end of the island, with your head swimming with unforgettable images and the knowledge that there's so much more to explore on this special island.

Beautiful Bike Rides for Every Ability

THE CAMDEN-ROCKPORT AREA ABOUNDS IN TRAILS for virtually every biking skill level and interest, from easy glides along the harbors to challenging mountain trails that'll test even the most proficient expert.

At the Camden Snow Bowl, about three miles west of town on the Barnestown Road, there are several miles of single-track mountain-biking trails maintained by the Mid Coast Maine Chapter of the New England Mountain Bike Association. Three well-marked trails start at the base of the ski area, ranging in difficulty from the 3.5-mile advanced Pitch Pole loop that climbs more than 600 vertical feet to the top of the chairlift, to the half-mile Chute loop that's perfect for beginners. An intermediate circuit, the Jibe Trail is about 1.5 miles long and climbs about 300 vertical feet. You can see all the details at www.camdensnowbowl.com/mountain-biking.

Camden Hills State Park, about three miles north of town on Route 1, also has mountain-biking trails for every skill level. The easiest, and most popular, is the appropriately named Multi-use Trail, which is also used by hikers and horseback riders—not to mention cross-country skiers in the winter. It's five miles of a relatively flat, well-graveled and graded double-track surface running from the camping area on Route 1 to a parking area on Route 173 between Lincolnville Center and Lincolnville Beach. At its midpoint is a recently completed replica of a ski lodge that was constructed some seventy years ago by the Civilian Conservation Corps at the base of a now-overgrown ski trail that is still open for hikers. Birds and wildlife abound on this pleasant ride through mixed forests and adjacent bogs.

Three other trails are open in the park for mountain bikers, and the most technical riders will head for the two-mile Frohock Mountain Trail, off the Multi-use Trail, to test their skills on a challenging surface of rocks and roots working their way up and down some steep slopes on three mountain peaks and through mixed oak and spruce forests.

And for those who like to spend a day pedaling their road bikes, I can't think of a better area than Camden-Rockport. To start planning, pick up a copy of the Camden Hiking and Biking Trail Map produced by the folks at Map Adventures: www.mapadventures.com. You'll find complete descriptions of a variety of interesting routes, ranging from a twenty-two-mile circuit of Megunticook Lake to what, for me, is the perfect ride along the shore of Penobscot Bay with abounding views of the Maine coast at its best.

This route is referred to as Beauchamp Point in the aforementioned map, and its 8.4-mile circuit is well-marked. I always make a counter-clockwise circuit starting right at the public landing in Camden heading toward Rockport on Bay View Street past the Camden Yacht Club. A short distance along you'll pass Laite Memorial Beach—keep this in mind, as you might want to return for a dip when your ride is finished—and you'll stay on Bay View Street for a 1.5-mile flat and winding ride to its intersection with Chestnut Street. Along the way you'll catch glimpses of Curtis Island guarding Camden Harbor, and other views across the bay to Vinalhaven and North Haven Islands.

Turning left on Chestnut Street, you'll soon be treated to the sight of Belted Galloway "Oreo Cookie" cows grazing in a field that runs down to Lily Pond at the Maine Coast Heritage Trust's Aldemere Farm.

Then turn left down Calderwood Lane, past the Megunticook Golf Club and around Beauchamp Point. You'll be tempted to spend a few minutes in the quiet seclusion of the Children's Chapel before continuing up the north side of Rockport Harbor along Beauchamp Avenue and into the village of Rockport.

Return to Camden on Union Street along the traffic-free Union Street Pathway, passing under the historic archway marking the border between Camden and Rockport. All told, there are enough biking options within a few miles of each other to satisfy every member of your family on multiple visits.

Down East Getaway

IF YOU'D LIKE TO SNEAK AWAY FOR THREE OR FOUR DAYS on a getaway that includes virtually every possible Maine summer delight, and even a visit to another country, here's a suggestion that has been a tradition for our family several times a summer for more years than I care to count.

It includes, among other things, hiking, camping, kayaking, biking, golfing, puffin spotting, whale watching, and international travel . . . all within four hours of our mid-coast Maine home.

Just head east on Route 1 until you reach tiny East Machias, where you'll turn right on Route 191, and follow the bay down to Cutler. There, your getaway starts with a trip out to Machias Seal Island with Captain Andrew Patterson of the Bold Coast Charter Company to see the largest puffin colony on the Maine coast. You'll not only see these unusual birds, you'll see them up close, which is a special experience.

Back on the road and following Route 191, about halfway between East Machias and Lubec, you'll reach the parking lot for the Cutler Coast Unit of the Maine Bureau of Parks and Lands for your first hike. This 12,000-acre paradise includes the best of everything you'd expect to find in Washington County: blueberry barrens, peat bogs, forested ledges, thick woods, grasslands, and meadows. But the real reason to hike is the steep, jagged cliffs that tower above the ocean along 4.5 miles of completely undeveloped coastline. There are two loops, one 5.8 miles and the other 9.8 miles, both of which are great hikes, but you can experience the best of the area by following the trail for about a mile and a half, right down to the cliffs, with a view of Grand Manan Island, New Brunswick, then return on the same trail back to your car. This is our customary choice, and the shorter hike gives us more time to cram in everything we want to do on our short getaway. If you do the longer loop, there are three remote and primitive tent sites out on Fairy Head that you might consider for an overnight.

Once back on Route 191, keep your eye out for Back Cove Road on the right that will take you past the trailheads for several more delightful hikes in the network that make up the Cobscook Trails. Boot Head Preserve and Hamilton Cove Preserve are both rewarding short hikes. If you don't do them on your first visit, make a note to include them on your next.

Next, continue along to the famed red and white striped West Quoddy Head lighthouse, perched on America's easternmost point of land. There, in 532-acre Quoddy Head State Park, you'll find more trails leading along the bold outcroppings above the ocean and another view over Grand Manan Channel.

Then it's back through Lubec. With new little shops, places to eat, and other attractions, Lubec is experiencing a renaissance of sorts since the demise of the sardine canning industry that fueled its early growth. Here you'll embark on your international travels as you cross the short bridge and pass through Canadian Customs (don't forget your passport) on to Campobello Island, New Brunswick.

Enough off the beaten path that it never gets crowded, the island is perhaps most famous as the site of FDR's family home and the 2,800 acre Roosevelt Campobello International Park. The residence, a magnificent thirty-four-room "cottage," where President Roosevelt spent many enjoyable summer vacations away from Washington, is the centerpiece of the park. It stands as both a memorial and a symbol of the close friendship between Canada and the United States, and both countries share in the funding, staffing, and administration of the park.

Once on the island, head for Herring Cove Provincial Park to set up your camp in the quiet seclusion of one of the campground's eighty-eight sites, or, if the weather's bad, take one of the four "canopies," enclosed shelters with bunks. Over many years of camping there, we've never had a problem picking out just the right site. Adding to the charm of the park is a crescent-shaped sand and pebble beach over a mile long, where a dozen people constitute a crowd, and there are plenty of biking opportunities both in the park, all over the island, and on the three carriage roads in the International Park. So be sure to bring along your bikes.

Bring your golf clubs along too, if that's your game, as there's a manicured, Geoffrey Cornish-designed nine-hole track that plays to over 6,000 yards with its second nine tees, and it gets about as crowded, in my experience, as the beach. In fact, I remember a round a couple of summers ago in the late evening (set your clocks back, it's Atlantic Time there, so the sun sets at about 10 p.m. in June) when my wife and I were the only two people on the entire course. The view from the first tee is one you'll never forget.

And pack the kayaks as well. Although the tides and currents around the island can be a little intimidating, you'll find great paddling in Mill Cove near the north end of the island. As a special reward for a visit to Mill Cove, sand dollars seem to have a special affinity for the beach there.

You'll want to hike the variety of trails on the island, and my favorite is the two-and-a-half-mile stretch between Raccoon Point and Liberty Point on the bold east shore in the International Park. Once at Liberty Point you may spot whales offshore—a pod of Minkes glided by us on our visit there.

At low tide, head for the lighthouse at East Quoddy Head, as you can hike out to it only at low tide. But you have to include a visit there for both its beauty and the opportunity to spot more whales. Whale watching tours are available out of Head Harbor, near the lighthouse, and on one of those you're virtually assured of sightings. It's also a great place to search for sea glass.

A special place to eat on island is the year-round seafood institution called Family Fisheries. Billed as a true Maritime dining adventure, I'll attest to that representation, proven on multiple visits there over the past twenty years. Lunch and dinner are also served at the golf course Club House, and there's another breakfast and lunch opportunity in a reopened bakery near the provincial park, which makes a nice alternative to campsite-prepared breakfasts. Especially after several days of camping.

Your getaway can best be concluded by picking the one alternate route off the island, the quirky M.V. Island Hopper ferry to Deer Island, New Brunswick. Eleven trips a day leave on the hour for a modest fare, car and all, and once on Deer Island, a drive to its north end takes you to the free government ferry to the mainland and the village of L'Etete, near St. George.

From there it's a short drive to scenic and historic St. Andrews, then a hop to St. Stephen and the border crossing back into Maine in Calais.

Believe me, you can cram more fun into three or four days there than almost any place I can think of, and it's not that far away.

Information, maps, pics:

www.campobello.com
www.fdr.net
www.maine.gov

Wondrous Waterfalls

GIVEN THE NUMBER OF STREAMS AND RIVERS IN MAINE, it should come as no surprise that there are dozens of spectacular waterfalls throughout the state. Interestingly, however, many folks I talk to have seen none, or only a few, of them.

Piscataquis, Oxford, Franklin, and Somerset Counties feature the preponderance of them, but the expanse of those four counties covers a pretty big chunk of Maine.

At 108 feet, Katahdin Stream Falls in Baxter State Park holds the record as Maine's highest waterfall, but over the years I've found enough waterfalls to fill several photo albums. These falls range from enchanting curtains no higher than ten feet to crashing torrents approaching ninety feet. Narrowing down the list to a few recommendations is tough, and the criteria I'll use is a combination of beauty and accessibility. The four I've chosen, which I visit every summer, require only a short hike or virtually no hike at all, as they're visible right from your vehicle.

Two must-see falls, which at ninety feet are in a virtual tie for second place in the "Highest Maine Waterfall" category, are Angel Falls in Township D in Franklin County, between Oquossoc and Mexico (on page 18, B-4, in the *DeLorme Atlas and Guide*), and Moxie Falls up in Moxie Gore, near The Forks south of Jackman (on page 40, E-3). Both require a short, but easy hike from the road on well-marked trails, although the hike in to Angel Falls requires you to ford a stream that, in the spring, is sometimes uncrossable, as I found on my first trip there several years ago. So you might plan to visit Angel Falls in the fall. Another, equally important, reason to hit Angel Falls in autumn is that the drive between Mexico and

Oquossoc on Route 17 during foliage season is to die for. Eating your lunch at the height of land overlooking Mooselookmeguntic Lake is about as good as it gets.

Angel Falls is so-named because when the flow is just right, an angel appears. And the flow is enhanced by the fact that the water plunges in tiers through a twenty-five-foot-wide gap in the rocks. To reach the falls, proceed 17.8 miles north of the intersection of Routes 2 and 17 in Mexico. You'll see an unmarked road on the left, and a small bridge is visible. Turn there and proceed 3.6 miles, where you'll see another unmarked road to the left, which goes down a steep hill and ends in a parking lot with a large boulder. From there it's a short hike of twenty to thirty minutes on a well-marked trail, across the aforementioned brook.

Moxie Falls is on Moxie Stream, about five miles southeast of the Kennebec River, popular for whitewater kayaking and rafting. You reach it by taking Route 201 north out of Skowhegan. Follow it up through Bingham and Caratunk until you reach The Forks. Turning right onto the Lake Moxie Road, and you'll reach the well-marked trailhead on the left after a couple of miles.

Many people say that Moxie Falls is unmatched in New England for its rugged beauty. There are also smaller unnamed cascades above and below the main falls, many large pools, including a great one for swimming about 100 feet downstream from the falls. The trail is about a mile long and about halfway in you'll see signs warning you to be watchful of changing water levels. The dam on Moxie Pond is occasionally opened to release water, substantially increasing the flow and the associated danger. It's a scramble down about a hundred feet to the base of the falls, and I do not recommend this climb for children. There are, however, some nice platforms along the trail from which to view the falls.

While you're up in that part of the state, consider paddling around relatively undeveloped Moxie Pond, or taking the short hike up Mosquito Mountain on the pond's west shore. There are great views of the Longfellow Mountains to the west from the summit.

Screw Auger Falls in Grafton Notch State Park is reachable on Route 26, which leaves Route 2 about three miles east of Bethel. There are signs to direct you to the park. The thirty-foot falls are about four miles east of the height of land in Grafton Notch. This waterfall is visible from the road, so it's a popular place to stop for lots of people, and you'll seldom have the falls to yourself. Regardless, you'll be rewarded with a memorable view

of banded granite formations through which the Bear River has carved its
intricate path over the centuries.

My fourth favorite Maine waterfall is Smalls Falls, on the upper reaches of
the fast-flowing Sandy River, on Route 4 just north of Madrid and south
of Rangeley. A favorite day trip takes us up through Grafton Notch by
Screw Auger Falls to Errol, New Hampshire, then back into Maine on
Route 16 through Oquossoc and Rangeley. It's a day-long excursion, but
you'll be able to see two of Maine's premier waterfalls while barely leaving
your vehicle.

There's a short boardwalk leading from the Smalls Falls Rest Area.
You'll come upon a three-foot cascade leading into a twenty-foot wide
wading pool, above which is a fourteen-foot fanning horsetail with a deep
pool at its base. You'll often see people (not me) jumping off the ledges
into this inviting pool. A short distance farther there's a twenty-five-foot
segmented waterfall, and beyond it a final one of about twelve feet, which
even features a natural water slide.

Consider at some point roaming farther afield and deeper into the
woods to visit Gulf Hagas—the Grand Canyon of Maine—Houston Brook
Falls in Pleasant Ridge Township, or Mad River Falls up in Batchelders
Grant.

For descriptions, maps, and photos of more of Maine's waterfalls, visit
www.newenglandwaterfalls.com.

Biking the Casco Bay Islands

YOU CAN KEEP YOUR CAR FERRIES AND SEGWAYS—for my money, one of the best ways to tour the Calendar Islands is by bike.

Casco Bay is dotted with hundreds of islands. So many, in fact, that an English engineer quipped in the 1700s that there were "as many islands as there are days in the year." The number has since been revised down to a bit less than 200, a nevertheless impressive count.

Fall is that magic period between summer crowds and winter cold, and in September and October, the roads on the islands offer a perfect combination of scenic views, warm temperatures, and low traffic. Only a few miles from Portland, it's easy to feel like you've discovered your own private island as you cruise around on two wheels.

The relatively flat terrain and small size of the islands—the largest, Chebeague, is just 3.2 square miles—means that even novice cyclists can tour the bay. Occasional rough patches and dirt roads make a hybrid or mountain bike advisable, but the grades are slight enough that you won't even need a cycle with multiple gears.

At only a fifteen-minute ferry ride from Portland (with more than a dozen Casco Bay Lines departures a day), Peaks Island is undoubtedly the easiest island to reach.

The second-largest island in Casco Bay, 720-acre Peaks is home to roughly 1,000 year-round residents—a number that swells significantly in summer. The island offers a perfect mix of beauty and convenience for cyclists, with a town on the west side and unobstructed ocean views on the east.

The Peaks Island Loop, part of the Portland Trails network, is a four-mile trek along paved roads that circle the island. Starting with a right turn up the hill from the island's ferry terminal, the route follows Island and Seashore Avenues.

After half a mile, you leave the "urban" (using the term very loosely) part of Peaks at Woodlanding Cove, and follow the rocky shore and beaches looking out to the Atlantic. The road sticks to the coast for about two miles, and a short hill by Elm Tree Cove is followed by a left turn steering back through town.

No bike? No worries. Peaks is also home to Brad & Wyatt's Bike Shop, where you can pick up a bike for just $5 an hour. The honor system box at the shop is a sign of Brad's and Wyatt's good natures—if no one is there to help you out, stuff your payment in the box and grab a bike. Also available at the shop are maps that offer a few more routes than the Island Loop.

A trip to Chebeague can be short or long, depending on your approach. A ferry ride from Portland with Casco Bay Lines takes about an hour and a half, and drops you at a ferry terminal on Chebeague's south end. The more expensive Chebeague Transportation ferry departs from Yarmouth, but deposits you on the island's north end after only fifteen minutes.

Your point of contact with Chebeague doesn't really matter, because your plan of attack is the same either way. A loop around the island is made by the appropriately named North and South Roads. Riding this loop is about a six-mile round-trip when you include the spur to and from either ferry terminal.

Your trip will be made slightly longer, however, by the many dirt roads leading to the island's shore.

The loop is pleasant, but restricts you largely to the interior of the island. To reach the myriad public beaches, you must explore the paths that lead off the paved road every few hundred yards.

My favorite? The beach at Indian Point on Chebeague's southwest tip, which has surprisingly blue waters and high dune grass for a beach in Maine.

There are plenty of trails on the mainland, but if you're looking for some great biking, I suggest heading out to sea.

Portland Beaches—by Bicycle

I N PORTLAND, WE'RE LUCKY ENOUGH to have the city's East End
Beach, as well as miles of spectacular sand beaches just across the Casco
Bay Bridge. In South Portland, Cape Elizabeth, and Scarborough, it's
an ideal spot between the rocky Down East coast and the commercial
blight of some southern Maine and New Hampshire beaches.

Though all the beaches in the Portland area are accessible by car, many
intrepid Portlanders have discovered how easy it is to reach them via bicycle. Willard Beach, Crescent Beach, Kettle Cove, and Higgins Beach are
all a short ride from the city. It's a lovely way to hit the beach; the roads
are well-maintained, an ocean breeze keeps riders cool, and bikes negate
the parking headaches that mount during the summer.

Distances are approximate from the Ocean Gateway ferry terminal. A
number of parking lots and garages surround the terminal, so you can easily
find a place to switch from car to bike. It's a straight shot up Commercial
Street from the terminal to the Casco Bay Bridge, the main thoroughfare
for bikers and motorists traveling to the beaches.

Willard Beach

At just under four miles from downtown Portland, Willard Beach is the
closest sand beach to the city. After crossing the Casco Bay Bridge, cyclists
take a left onto the Greenbelt Trail and follow the smooth, paved path to
Bug Light and the Southern Maine Community College campus. A right
turn onto Breakwater Drive completes the trip to the beach.

The four-acre beach, situated between SMCC and Fisherman's Point,
is one of the most popular in South Portland. During the summer season,

restrooms, a snack bar, and a bathhouse and showers are available. A short trip north along the shore takes you to Bug Light Park, with views of both the lighthouse and the city of Portland. Parking is free for cyclists or motorists.

Crescent Beach State Park and Kettle Cove

Located on Seal Cove in Cape Elizabeth, Crescent Beach State Park is a 7.5-mile ride from Portland proper. After crossing the Casco Bay Bridge, a right turn onto Route 77 (Ocean Street) gives you a direct path to the beaches. Five miles from the bridge, the road splits—a left turn onto Ocean House Road leads to Kettle Cove, while continuing on Route 77 brings you to Crescent Beach.

Crescent Beach is an oddity in Maine, at least north of Old Orchard— a mile-long flat, sandy beach with light surf and sun-warmed water. Like Willard Beach, the park offers bathhouses, restrooms, and a snack bar, along with grills and picnic tables. Entrance to the state park is $4.50 for Maine residents and $6.50 for nonresidents.

Kettle Cove tends to offer a slightly less crowded beach experience, with most of the car and foot traffic funneled to Crescent. Easy hiking trails connect Kettle to Maxwell and John Coves. The parking lot at Kettle fills up much more quickly than Crescent, however, but cyclists don't have to worry about finding a place to park.

If you want to make a loop of the beaches, it's six miles from Willard Beach to the state park. Simply follow the scenic Shore Road past Fort Williams Park and Portland Head Light, connecting back to Route 77 after a few miles.

Higgins Beach

The farthest beach from downtown Portland on this tour, Higgins Beach is about nine miles from the city. After crossing the Casco Bay Bridge, turn right onto Route 77 (Ocean Street) for just over a mile. A right turn onto Spurwink Avenue takes you the remaining five miles to Ocean Avenue, the street that connects to Higgins Beach.

Scarborough's Higgins Beach is quaint compared to the other area beaches, with no facilities available for visitors. It's a beautiful half-mile sand beach, and the historic homes and seaside cottages that abut the sand make for a scenic backdrop. Of note on the beach are the remains of the *Howard W. Middleton*, a three-masted schooner that wrecked in the late

1800s. Not much of the ship remains, but the ribs of the hull still stick out like ancient fossils.

Motorists must pay to park in the Higgins Beach lot, but cyclists can park for free.

For cyclists making a beach loop, it's four miles from Crescent Beach to Ocean Avenue. The path is an easy one—simply stay on Route 77 until you see Ocean on your left. A nine-mile trip back to Portland makes the loop of the four beaches a twenty-four-mile round-trip.

Rock Climbing
Up, Up, and Away

Though I'm a lifelong hiker and skier—meaning I'm definitely not risk-averse—I've never been able to take the leap into serious rock climbing.

Rock climbing, a sport practiced around the world for ages, has exploded in popularity over the last decade. Much of this growth has coincided with the construction of indoor rock gyms, like Maine Rock Gym in Portland and the facilities near Sugarloaf and Sunday River. As gym climbers gain skills inside year-round, they naturally want to take their climbs into the great outdoors. And Maine has plenty of features to appeal to novice and expert climbers, from seaside bluffs to massive inland mountains.

Looking into climbing, my first concern was simpler than cost, risk, or equipment: Am I even fit enough to go rock climbing? Jon Tierney, owner of Acadia Mountain Guides and a licensed climbing instructor, assured me that climbing is within reach of pretty much anyone. "Going up stairs or a ladder is climbing," he reminded me, "so that is a good benchmark." Like traditional hiking, there's a range of difficulty in climbing.

Obviously, if you'd like to scale a sheer 2,000-foot face, you'll need to be a bit more toned than if you'd like to complete a novice climb. But for the most part, if you're in decent shape, climbing is within reach. So, great news. If you're fit, you can climb. How about cost?

"The initial investment is fairly low to climb inside," said Chuck Curry of Portland's Maine Rock Gym. A harness and climbing shoes cost in the neighborhood of $140, and the typical rock gym membership still will keep you under $200. A month at MRG, for example, costs $54.50.

Climbing outside requires more equipment and thus a little more expense. A harness, chalk, belay devices, rope and anchor gear, and other accoutrements make rock climbing a bit more costly. However, for bouldering—short climbs without ropes—shoes, chalk, and a crash pad are all a climber needs.

Both Tierney and Curry stress that while it is possible to teach yourself to climb, it's a better idea to learn from a professional. Most importantly, you're much safer in the hands of a professional. As easy as it may seem to get started climbing, it can be a sport of high consequence if you make an error. Under the watchful eye of an instructor or guide, you can advance light-years beyond what you would achieve on your own in a fraction of the time.

It's not unlike learning to ski or sail—while you can figure plenty out on your own, a knowledgeable instructor corrects misconceptions about the sport, fills gaps in knowledge, and progresses you in a sensible way.

Both Maine Rock Gym and Acadia Mountain Guides offer a wide range of lessons for first-time and experienced climbers. MRG offers indoor climbing clinics for all skill levels, as well as a guide service that facilitates people climbing outside. AMG hosts classes for rock, ice, and mountaineering throughout the year, with family climbs, private guiding, and Katahdin winter ascents being among the most popular.

The climbing enthusiasts I spoke with pointed to a number of reasons that Maine is a great place to pick up the sport. Key among these is diversity. In Acadia National Park, there are dozens of climbing routes with fantastic coastal views. While a hike up Precipice will net some impressive sights, they can't quite compare to the perspective from the classic "Old Town" and "Return to Forever" ascents—two that Curry names as favorites. Clifton, east of Bangor, is also a haven for climbers.

Farther inland, Katahdin offers summer routes that Tierney compares with "the Tetons without the altitude." In the winter, Katahdin hosts a mix of rock, ice, and snow climbs that range from 200 to 2,000 feet. In the western mountains and along the New Hampshire border, climbers pour superlatives on routes that offer technical difficulty and are far enough from urban centers to keep crowds at bay.

There are even some dedicated climbers who go bouldering on the rocks at Nubble, Portland Head Light, and other Maine lighthouses.

Climbing is one of the great year-round athletic pursuits, be it scaling summer rocks and winter ice or climbing 365 days a year at an indoor gym. With the modest investment and huge returns, rock climbing is yet another way that all Mainers can get a stunning new perspective on our state.

Tunk Mountain

FOR COUNTLESS YEARS (DECADES, IN FACT) I often thought, as I followed Route 182 from Hancock to Cherryfield on my forays Down East, that Tunk Mountain was beckoning to me. With its ledgy summit ridge and obviously outstanding views, and as the northerly sister to scenic Schoodic Mountain, I was determined to one day find my way to the top. Up until a couple of years ago, only local cognoscenti knew both where to park and how to find a route to the top.

All that changed when the Maine Bureau of Parks and Lands built a parking lot some fourteen miles east of the intersection of Routes 1 and 182 in Hancock, on what is now identified as the Black Woods Scenic Byway. A large informational kiosk helps hikers find trails both to the top and around some ponds. A pit toilet is conveniently located there as well.

In addition to the 1,157-foot mountain, the entire 6,915-acre addition to the Donnell Pond Public Reserved Lands Unit includes several small ponds, Spring River Lake, and the north and east shores of Tunk Lake.

You'll spot the well-marked parking area on the left less than a mile past little Fox Pond, which is on the right side of the the road.

From the parking lot, the trail winds through a quiet mixed forest, star-tlingly peppered with impressive glacial boulders. In the wetter softwood stands, bog bridges have been constructed to make the hike easier . . . and drier.

After about half a mile, the unmarked south end of the Hidden Ponds Loop Trail joins from the right. I bypassed this to continue on the main Tunk Mountain Trail. A short distance farther you pass along the west shore of Salmon Pond before coming to the intersection of the north end of the Loop Trail. If weather, or your courage, suggests that a walk around the one-mile loop with views of Salmon and Little Long Ponds might be better than an assault of Tunk, returning to your car via that route is a delightful option.

If you opt to continue to the summit ridge, you'll pass an attractive little pond, inappropriately named Mud Pond. Over the decades, I've been on many of the countless Mud Ponds that dot Maine's backcountry, and most of them live up to that name. This one, however, is almost alpine in character, as ledges drop directly down into the water. It looked to me like a haven for some brookies, but I later learned that the pond's high acidity has rendered it fish-less.

The trail begins to rise over a series of ridges, and across a couple of musical streams with one featuring a photogenic waterfall. About 1.3 miles from the trailhead, an expansive vista opens up to the east, with views down to the ponds below, hills beyond them, and the Down East coast in the distance.

A moderately strenuous climb, including a rung-assisted section, as you get nearer the ridge, is rewarded with a second ledgy vista, near which a plaque commemorating the benefactors responsible for this public treasure is set in a stone.

Upon reaching the ridge, the trail turns north to a craggy viewpoint. The pristine scene interrupted—in the eyes of staunch preservationists—by a wind farm on a hill a few miles away

The entire hike, if you decide to climb to the summit, and then take the Hidden Ponds Loop, as I did, on the return trip, totals a little less than five miles. At my pace, having gotten on the trail at about 8:30 a.m., I was back at the trailhead by 11 a.m. Only one other hiker was on the trail during my walk, so it felt almost as if I were on my own private preserve.

This left time for a couple of more treats on my outing. First, I had noted a convenient, although unmarked, launch site right at the east end of Fox Pond, so popping the kayak into the water was unavoidable. An hour paddling around the rocky shoreline was a great way to give my upper body a little workout and, needless to say, rest my legs before the drive home.

Second, it was time for lunch when I got to Jordan's Snack Bar in Ellsworth—not that I hadn't planned it that way—and the fried clams and onion rings that I had been thinking about on my way up Tunk Mountain were just as good as they've always been, and I knew they would be.

Spectacular Schoodic Peninsula

A LESS-FREQUENTED, BUT NONETHELESS SPECTACULAR section of Acadia National Park lies about an hour's drive east of Mt. Desert Island on the other side of Frenchman Bay. There the Schoodic Peninsula is home to the only portion of Acadia on the mainland of Maine, featuring granite headlands, rocky beaches, and spruce-fir forests.

In fact, many of us feel that the Schoodic section of the park contains within its more than 2,000 acres all of the very best that the coast of Maine has to offer. Added to the beauty is the opportunity to combine three summertime recreational diversions in the same day: biking, hiking, and kayaking.

You get to the peninsula by driving east on Route 1 from Ellsworth through Hancock and Sullivan, then turning down Route 186 in West Gouldsboro for the short, scenic drive to Winter Harbor and into the park.

During the summer months a small ferry plies the waters between Bar Harbor and Winter Harbor, and you can then hop on an Island Explorer bus (free) to tour the peninsula, which also includes Birch Harbor and Prospect Harbor. The bus leaves from the ferry terminal in Bar Harbor for folks who want to leave the driving to them.

Your biking adventure should begin at the Frazer Point picnic area just after you enter the park, at which point you'll embark on a one-way six-mile portion of the Park Loop Road that'll take you along the ocean's edge to Schoodic Point with its often dramatic surf (Note: Use caution on the slippery rocks of the point. People have been swept off the ledges when the waves are particularly high.)

The speed limit for automobiles is just thirty-five mph on the one-way section of road, and cars are usually going even slower than that as people drink in the scenery, so it's a safe ride.

Continuing on the road after it becomes two-way in Wonsqueak Harbor, it's on to Birch Harbor, then back to Winter Harbor on Route 186. In recent years, a bike lane has been added to this section, vastly improving what at one time was a kind of dicey ride.

Once back to your car at Frazer Point, where there are tables, fire rings, restrooms, and drinking water, you can begin your kayaking fun. Although there are no designated launch sites in the park, there's a tiny beach right next to the pier at the picnic area that's easy to access, and you can pop your kayak in there. Another option is to launch at the public site in Winter Harbor, but from there it's a pretty long paddle out around the point, so you might save that for a day when you want to spend all your time out on the water.

A perfect place to launch is at a little side road 2.3 miles along the road from Frazer Point. There's even enough space to park your car well off the road. As you proceed along the one-way road, you'll see a rocky berm leading out to Pond Island, and just past there, in a quiet cove, you'll spot the site. From there I launched on one delightful paddle and circumnavigated Pond Island, went out around the point, and explored the shoreline of Little Moose Island. Farther beyond, Schoodic Island and Rolling Island lie beckoning, but bear in mind they are both closed from February 15 through August 31 to protect nesting birds.

So after a couple of hours on the bike and a few in the kayak, you're ready for the hiking segment of the day. Lest you think this sounds overly ambitious, I hasten to add that the biking is mostly on easy grades, and the hike is short and relatively easy.

There are four interconnecting trails, and your destination is 440-foot Schoodic Head, which has commanding views of the peninsula and ocean. Starting at the Blueberry Hill parking area, head out on the 0.6-mile easy Alder Trail though a shrubland, then up the moderate 0.6-mile Schoodic Head Trail to the summit. From there it's down the 1.1-mile Anvil Trail with a few steep sections back to the Loop Road at a point very close to your car.

The fourth trail is the short half-mile East Trail that leaves the road less than a mile beyond the Blueberry Hill parking lot and reaches the summit in about a half mile over some fairly steep terrain.

Of course, it's not a requisite for you to do all three on your trip. Combining two of the activities, or even doing only one, is still a great way to experience the park.

The Wonderful Abundance of Port Clyde

S ITUATED ON THE SOUTHERNMOST TIP of the St. George Peninsula, the scenic mid-coast community of Port Clyde is a haven for bikers, beachgoers, and kayakers.

Short of a chartered boat or ferry, the only way to reach Port Clyde is to take Route 131 south from Thomaston. It's a winding and narrow road, but one that's been well-maintained over the years. With ample parking available in Thomaston, the best way to experience the trip down the peninsula is by bicycle.

The first bit of the ride is a bit discouraging—an unrelenting, nearly mile-long climb from downtown Thomaston that passes the regal General Henry Knox Museum. Once you crest the hill, however, the fourteen miles to Port Clyde are mostly flat.

The route takes cyclists through St. George and Tenants Harbor, seaside communities bursting with New England charm. Route 131 rarely leaves sight of the water, and Cutler, Watts, and Seavey Coves provide natural air-conditioning on even the hottest days.

In Port Clyde, the biggest tourist attraction is undoubtedly Marshall Point Light. Constructed in 1832 to mark the entrance to Port Clyde Harbor, the granite and brick lighthouse is among the oldest in the state. It's also one of the most photographed lighthouses in New England, in no small part due to the unique wooden bridge connecting the light to the shore. The spot is a favorite of storytellers as well, most famously acting as the eastern terminus of Tom Hanks's cross-country run in *Forrest Gump*.

The grounds of the lighthouse are open daily from dawn until dusk. The building, originally the keeper's quarters, now houses a gift shop and a museum. Both are open daily during the summer. The grounds are a one-mile walk from downtown Port Clyde, but there is plenty of parking at the lighthouse for those who would rather drive.

Just north of the lighthouse on Drift Inn Road, the Drift-In Beach is a secret haven for mid-coast beach dwellers. It's a small beach, only about a quarter-mile long, but it's one of the few sand beaches north of Old Orchard. The gentle slope of the sand means that, at low tide, acres of beach seem to spread in front of you. The combination of sand and shallows also means that the high sun of summer warms the water significantly. A jump in the ocean at Drift-In is a bit less shocking than in other places.

There is a small parking lot next to the beach, but it fills up quickly during the summer. Not a problem if you rode your bike to Port Clyde, but drivers may be stuck parking on the side of the road and hoofing it back to the beach.

From the calm waters of Port Clyde Harbor, sea kayakers can explore the coves and islands of the Maine coast. This stretch of the coastline is thick with wildlife, and it's not uncommon to spot seals, porpoises, osprey, and eagles. A local outfitter, Port Clyde Kayaks, offers guided tours and instruction for those who aren't interested in striking out on their own.

If paddle power doesn't interest you, the Monhegan Boat Line in Port Clyde offers ferry service to Monhegan Island. The trip to the island makes for a wonderful single- or multiday excursion, especially for hikers. While hiking trails are few and far between around Port Clyde, Monhegan has more than seventeen miles of trails along cliff, shore, and forest.

The Port Clyde area is nationally known as a haven for artists and photographers, and with good reason. The town, the lighthouse, and the surrounding coves and islands are among the most scenic in a state with no shortage of breathtaking scenery. Hiking, biking, and kayaking around the area puts you right in the thick of things, closer than armchair visitors could dream to be.

St. Andrews By-The-Sea

A SCANT HALF-HOUR DRIVE EAST OF THE BORDER crossing between Calais and St. Stephen in New Brunswick sits one of Canada's oldest and best-preserved eighteenth-century towns and the country's oldest seaside resort.

St. Andrews by-the-Sea, as it's known throughout the world, has been designated a National Historic District, and a visit to the quaint New England-style village, with its compact and neatly organized business district bordering Passamaquoddy Bay, easily confirms why so many people include St. Andrews in their Canadian travel itinerary.

We discovered the spot some twenty years ago when traveling to Fundy National Park for some camping with our sons, and now we can't resist a visit or two every summer. For us, it's a perfect spot to stop around lunchtime as we travel to Campobello Island, where we camp several times each summer. St. Andrews is on the way to a small ferry that runs from L'Etete to Deer Island to connect with another ferry to Campobello.

Only about three and a half hours from our mid-coast home via Route 9 to Calais, it's a nice alternative to driving Route 1 to Lubec and taking the bridge to New Brunswick, the route we usually take for our return home.

And there's something special about the connection between St. Andrews and Maine, as the town was settled by United Empire Loyalists in 1783 following the American Revolution. Several of them were residents of Castine, loyal to England and opposed to independence. They dismantled their homes and brought them in barges across the bay to reassemble them in Canada. Some of those houses still stand, making much of the compact residential district look much like the town from which the Loyalists emigrated. Many of the more than 250 homes are 200 years old and have been restored and marked with descriptive plaques by the St. Andrews Civic Trust.

The town's appeal is enhanced by the neatly squared off streets of the village center, carefully trimmed lawns, and splashes of color from the many gardens and brightly painted homes and commercial buildings.

It was at the beginning of the twentieth century that the town emerged as Canada's first seaside resort, to which many of the East's more prominent families were attracted. Some came to play golf at the eighteen-hole Algonquin Golf Course and to stay at the Algonquin Resort, now a Marriott property undergoing extensive upgrades and remodeling. The grand old hotel is the town's dominant landmark, spectacularly perched overlooking the peninsula.

When we can arrange it, we try to plan our visits on a Thursday, as that's the day the Farmers Market is held in Market Square in the center of town. Featuring far more than just native farm products, the weekly market runs from the end of May until mid-October. Booths filling the square present a variety of products, including preserves, home baking, crafts, woodworking, knitting, quilted goods, plants and flowers; and shoppers can browse to the accompaniment of live music.

Seafood restaurants abound in the downtown district, and a special favorite of ours is the Red Herring, with an outside deck overlooking the square and a beer batter-dipped haddock that's among my favorites.

The town dock is home port to several whale and wildlife spotting operations that take you out to experience whales, seals, porpoises, and a variety of seabirds in a setting that includes historic lighthouses and modern aquaculture operations.

There's also a launch site for your kayak, bikes for rent, and a trail up nearby Chamcook Mountain for a little exercise. And you can book a scuba-diving expedition to the teeming undersea life in area waters.

New in the past year is a boat running directly between St. Andrews and Campobello, run by the same enterprising entrepreneur who introduced guided tours of Campobello Island originating at the Roosevelt Cottage in the International Park on the island.

For youngsters, the Fundy Discovery Aquarium can be great fun, and the beach at Katy's Cove is the perfect spot for a dip in the chilly water of Passamaquoddy Bay.

Remember, passports are now required to reenter the United States from Canada, so be sure to bring yours along on what will prove a wonderful international excursion right in our own backyard.

So Many Adventures Await

S TANDING ATOP THE OLD STONE TOWER on the summit of Douglas Mountain, I was struck by the number of options before me. To the northwest I could see a handful of Maine's western mountains, along with the ghost of Mount Washington in the distance. To the east, late-season kayakers paddled on Sebago Lake. Beyond Sebago, cars streamed to Portland and Maine's coast.

Sometimes we can forget the bounty of options to explore the outdoors in our own backyard. More than any other place, Maine's mountains, ocean, rivers, and woodlands make for a playground that is not only varied but open year-round.

The allure isn't new. More than a century ago, it attracted Thoreau to "Ktaadn" and the northern forests. Today, Maine attracts over a million tourists every year. Though most are only summer visitors and some never leave the small cities and towns, many come to explore our backyard.

For outdoors lovers, the problem is that there are too many things to do, too many places to play, exercise, and explore. The thirty-two state parks, eighteen ski areas, and thousands of miles of trails to hike and bike offer more options than a staff of 100 outdoors writers could cover in a year.

This book has primarily covered the activities of hiking, biking, and paddling, and while this extensive coverage isn't a bad thing, it is a disservice to Maine's myriad other outdoor activities.

The odds are you haven't yet seen every inch of Maine on foot, bike, or boat. But let's say you have. Or let's say you're looking for something else to do outside during Maine's beautiful spring, summer, and fall weekends. Friend, I have you covered.

Surfing: Though many think of this as a Pacific sport, Maine has an active (and growing) surfing scene. Most of the activity is based on the southern coast from Ogunquit to Cape Elizabeth, where the state's rocky shores give way to sandy beaches. Thick wetsuits and all-weather gear even make year-round surfing a possibility here.

Maine's weather and frigid water can be punishing to new surfers, and it's not an easy sport to pick up on your own. Luckily, shops like Liquid Dreams and Aquaholics offer lessons and rentals, as well as equipment to buy. Another great resource is MaineWaves.com. Along with free maps, forecasts, and other tips, the site sells a comprehensive *Maine Surfer's Guidebook*, the "definitive guide for surfing the Maine coast."

Also worth mentioning is stand-up paddleboarding. A cousin to surfing, paddleboarding is basically what it sounds like: standing on a board and paddling. It's a full-body workout, great cross-training, and allows for boarding on lakes and streams as well as the ocean.

Suggested trip: Liquid Dreams, 171 Long Beach Ave., York. 207-351-2545.

Disc Golf: Replace the balls and holes of old-school golf with Frisbees and metal baskets, and you've got a whole new sport—disc golf. As in traditional golf, the aim of disc golf is to get from a tee to a hole in as few strokes (disc tosses) as possible, avoiding obstacles like water and trees. Also, like regular golf, disc golf is a great excuse to spend a few (sometime frustrating) hours in the great outdoors. Or as William Wordsworth put it, golf is "a day spent in a round of strenuous idleness."

Maine is home to more than two dozen disc golf courses, ranging from small eighteen-hole community courses to Randolph's massive fifty-four-hole, sixty-one-acre LaVallee Links. The PDGA—disc golf's version of the PGA—maintains a list of Maine's thirty-two courses at PDGA.com. Most of these courses have pro shops, where you can either buy or rent gear for the day. It's an easy sport to pick up without professional lessons, though it's difficult to master.

Suggested trip: Sabattus Disc Golf, 605 Bowdoinham Road, Sabattus. 207-375-4990.

Zip Lines and Rope Courses: First popularized as a tourist attraction in South America and New Zealand, zip lines are systems of cables and pulleys that propel visitors along by force of gravity. Step off a high platform while holding onto a pulley or wearing a harness, and zip along a line to a lower point.

A number of zip line parks have opened here in recent years, spanning from huge fabricated courses in southern Maine to lines that take riders over the rivers and through the woods of Maine's western mountains.

Courses in Windham, Saco, and Wiscasset mix zip lines with swinging beams, cargo nets, ladders, and other aerial obstacles. The courses run between $35 and $50 for a few hours of entertainment.

Suggested trip: Monkey C Monkey Do, 698 Bath Road (Route 1), Wiscasset. 207-882-6861.

Birding: Given Maine's location (we're precisely halfway between the North Pole and the equator) and the diverse ecology of its coast and interior, it is no surprise that the state is home to more than 330 bird species, from temporary migrants to year-round residents. It's always a delight to randomly spot a bird on the trail, but there's more fun to be had in dedicated birding.

The best point of ingress is the Maine Office of Tourism's "Maine Birding Trail" pamphlet. The guide (available for free at visitmaine.com) lists the best places around the state to spot birds, along with travel tips, the "Code of Birding Ethics," and a Maine birds checklist. With locations from Fort Foster to Aroostook State Park, the guide offers a great excuse to explore the entirety of Maine.

If you're particularly eagle-eyed, you may even spot a few species while surfing, disc golfing, or riding a zip line!

Suggested trip: Gilsland Farm Audubon Center, 20 Gilsland Farm Road, Falmouth. 207-781-2330.